Woman's Day
COOKING FOR ONE

Edited by Jeri Laber

Woman's Day
COOKING FOR ONE

◑⫯◑⫯◑⫯◑⫯◑⫯◑⫯◑⫯◑⫯◑⫯◑⫯◑⫯◑⫯◑⫯◑⫯◑⫯◑⫯◑⫯◑⫯

 Random House · New York

Library of Congress Cataloging in Publication Data
Main entry under title:
Woman's day cooking for one.
    Includes index.
    1.   Cookery.   I.   Laber, Jeri.   II.   Title: Cooking
for one.
TX652.W6618   641.5'61   77-90320
ISBN 0-394-41209-5

ILLUSTRATIONS BY LILLY LANGOTSKY

Manufactured in the United States of America
    4 5 6 7 8 9

CONTENTS

INTRODUCTION &ebd; vii

SOUPS &ebd; 3

SANDWICHES, HAMBURGERS AND FRANKS &ebd; 25

MEAT &ebd; 65

CHICKEN AND CHICKEN LIVERS &ebd; 103

FISH AND SHELLFISH &ebd; 123

VEGETABLES &ebd; 143

SALADS &ebd; 157

RICE AND PASTA &ebd; 175

SAUCES AND DRESSINGS &ebd; 191

EGGS AND CRÊPES &ebd; 205

DESSERTS &ebd; 225

INDEX &ebd; 243

INTRODUCTION by Jeri Laber

"WHAT'S THE POINT OF FUSSING OVER DINNER if it's just for me?" many people ask. The answer is very simple: single people need pampering too.

An uncommon number of them, including those who otherwise prefer a solitary life, dread mealtime. They find the very thought of dining alone boring at best, and at the very worst, exceedingly lonesome.

But that is because most single people don't treat themselves right. When mealtime rolls around, they simply settle for the first edible thing they see. More often than not, this means hastily prepared foods which are not only monotonous but nutritionally deficient as well.

But cooking for one can be rewarding and it can be fun, as this book will show you. Up to now, the problem has been that when you try to divide standard cookbook recipes to suit your smaller needs, the dish was often a disappointment. Proportions of ingredients frequently change when you divide a recipe, and cooking times change, too. It is also difficult to buy many types of food in small enough sizes or quantities. We know a single man who diligently cooks a large roast or turkey every Sunday, and then forces himself to eat the same thing every night of the week until the leftovers are gone. How boring! But if our friend had this book to show him how to plan, shop, cook and dine on a small, simple, yet wonderful scale, it would spare him dull, repetitive leftovers day after day.

Of course, when you are cooking just for yourself, the idea of slaving for hours over a hot stove is not very exciting. We know that and our recipes are realistic: easy to follow, requiring little time or patience. Though our soups, for example, are made from scratch, they can be fixed quickly and will be tasty and satisfying. We have a chapter on sandwiches, hamburgers and frankfurters—staples for the single person—which we elevate from the ordinary to something special. And don't think that because you live alone you have to skip homemade desserts. Everyone deserves desserts and you'll find them here, perfectly suited to those who are cooking for one.

Just think of the pleasures of eating alone. You never have to dress for dinner. If you feel like reading while you eat, or watching television, or playing the stereo—nobody is going to complain. You don't have to talk when you don't feel like it. And you never have to cook or eat something you do not like. You can follow your own preferences: buy and cook only the white meat of chicken, for example, if you don't like the dark. If someday you crave something which, when bought in quantity, is prohibitively expensive—scallops or shrimp, even lobster—you can probably afford to splurge, since it's just for you.

Make eating alone a pleasurable adventure. Set an attractive table for yourself—with candles and fresh flowers, a pretty placemat and nice dishes. Or vary your meals by eating in different parts of your home—sit by the fire or at the window, or if you're feeling lazy, fix yourself a luxurious "in bed" tray and truly relax. Be creative, not only in the way you present the food but in what you cook. Experiment with new dishes and new cooking techniques—after all, if you fail, the only person you can disappoint is yourself.

If you live alone, buy in small quantities. Economy-size items will not save you money if they are going to go stale while waiting to be used. Look for small sizes of everything—small onions, small garlic cloves, small canned goods (usually 8-ounce sizes). Buy coffee beans and grind them yourself; ground coffee loses flavor when it is stored for too long.

These recipes call for fresh ingredients wherever possible because they are tasty and nutritious. Also, you can buy a quarter pound, if that is all you need. Buying small quantities of meat may pose problems: supermarkets usually package meat in large quantities. But most markets will divide a package in half if you ask them to. The meat cutter will be more helpful if you shop at less busy times in the market.

A freezer, of course, will solve many problems. You can divide the meat yourself, and freeze what remains. Ground meat can be formed into patties, wrapped separately, and frozen. That way you will always have hamburgers on hand in exactly the right amount. Or if you have leftover cooked meat, slice it and wrap it in convenient portions.

The handiness of a freezer cannot be stressed enough. You can make a double recipe of one of your favorite dishes, then freeze half of it so that one day, when you are tired and hungry, all you have to do is reheat the prepared food—and dinner is ready! Freeze casserole-type dishes in aluminum or glass containers that can be taken straight from the freezer to a preheated oven. But take care not to use them directly on the top burners of your stove or under the broiler unless the manufacturer says that you can.

You can also pack cooked foods in freezer bags that can be submerged in boiling water when you are ready to reheat the food. This procedure is especially suitable for foods that might dry out in oven reheating.

When you are reheating frozen foods in the oven, it is usually a good idea to keep the temperature at 325° or 350° F. Bring the food to serving temperature, but take care not to overcook it. Keep food covered while reheating, unless you want it to be crisp.

Foods that might dry out in the oven should be reheated in a double boiler. If you do not own one, invent one. If you have a metal bowl that fits over the top of a saucepan, use that. Or try sticking a pie plate over a pot of boiling water and cover it with another, inverted pie plate.

Electric appliances are also handy for reheating frozen foods; toaster ovens, slow cookers or electric skillets are all good for that purpose.

Soups and stews can be stored in small coffee or peanut cans with tight-fitting lids or in sturdy, heavy-quality plastic containers. These containers can be put in a few inches of simmering water to speed up defrosting. Once the food becomes loose in the containers, it can be transferred to a covered pot for slow reheating.

Meat should be wrapped in heavy-duty aluminum foil

or heavy-weight plastic wrap for freezing; both are easier to use than freezer paper. Very small quantities of food, like egg whites or sauces or small amounts of stock, may be frozen in individual ice-cube trays or in small paper cups, covered with aluminum foil and secured with a rubber band.

The temperature of the freezer should be 0° F. or lower. Keep your freezer well organized and do not lose track of what you have there. Try to use items that have been there the longest, so the contents of the freezer continue to rotate. Always seal your containers well and label them with tape indicating the quantity of the contents and the date they were stored. Use masking tape for labeling instead of freezer tape; it is less expensive. Write with a pencil, a waterproof marking pen or with crayons. Regular ink will fade.

In equipping your cooking-for-one kitchen, think small. You will need several small saucepans, 1-quart and 2-quart sizes, and small and medium-sized skillets. A large pot is also handy for boiling corn, cooking spaghetti and, of course, for when you have guests. It is also helpful to own several small baking dishes in 10-ounce and 16-ounce sizes that can go directly from the freezer to the oven. For desserts for one, individual custard cups, single tart pans and a cookie sheet are nice to own.

Chances are your kitchen is fairly small; you need all the cooking space you have. If you own large electric appliances such as an electric mixer, why not store them away where they won't take up valuable working space? For your small needs, a wire whisk or rotary beater will beat eggs or cream. Or invest in a small hand-held electric mixer.

It is no fun trying to cook if you do not own the proper utensils; it becomes too frustrating. We have compiled a list of essentials that belong in every kitchen. It is short and does not pretend to be all-inclusive. Only *you* know what your kitchen needs really are. But no kitchen is complete without the following:

two or three sharp knives in different sizes
bread knife
knife sharpener
cutting board
wooden spoons
slotted spoon
metal spatula
two-tined fork
ladle
rubber spatula
a set of measuring spoons
measuring cups (1-cup and 2-cup sizes)
strainer
colander
grater and shredder
funnel
tongs
pepper mill
salt shaker
garlic press
corkscrew
can and bottle openers
apple parer and corer
potato peeler
juicer
grapefruit knife

rolling pin
meat and poultry thermometer
electric blender or food mill
small portable timer
small coffee pot

Whether you are retired, a student, recently divorced, a young single or a middle-aged widow, *Woman's Day Cooking for One* will show you how to bid goodbye to dreary solitary meals and start enjoying dining again. An attractive, delicious and nutritious meal for one, if you know how to prepare it, takes only a short time to assemble—and oh, what a difference a good meal can make!

Woman's Day
COOKING FOR ONE

SOUPS

✿⟩

❀❀❀❀❀❀❀❀❀❀❀❀❀❀❀❀❀❀❀❀❀❀❀❀❀❀❀

EAT A BOWL OF SOUP to whet your appetite, or include it in your meal to add substance when the meal seems a little light. Many soups are nourishing enough to stand on their own as a main course, with bread, cheese or a salad on the side. There are cold, refreshing soups for hot, muggy days, and soups that transcend the seasons, being equally good served hot or cold.

Each of these recipes will produce about 2 cups of soup, enough for seconds if it's your main course. There's no problem if it's not, however, since almost all soups keep well and often improve with age. And it's always nice to have a little leftover soup in the refrigerator for a satisfying midafternoon or late-evening snack.

Soups also freeze well. Just because you're only one, don't discount the many soups that are usually made in large quantities because they require long hours of simmering with bones and stock. Recipes for them are outside the scope of this cookbook, but there's no reason not to make such soups if you have proper freezer space: just package the finished soup in lots of one- or two-cup containers and freeze it for future use. If you don't have beef or chicken stock on hand, you can of course substitute canned broth when the recipe calls for stock or broth.

Oyster Stew

½ cup shucked oysters with liquid
1 cup milk or half-and-half
1 tablespoon butter
¼ teaspoon salt
Freshly ground pepper
Generous dash of cayenne
Minced parsley
Oyster crackers

Reserve the oysters and drain the liquid into a saucepan. Add the milk, butter, salt and pepper and cayenne to taste, and heat to the boiling point. Add the oysters and simmer just until the edges of the oysters curl; do not overcook. Garnish with parsley and eat with crackers. You will have about 2 cups.

Avocado Bisque

1 small ripe avocado, peeled and seeded
1½ teaspoons minced onion
1½ teaspoons butter
1½ teaspoons flour
1 cup chicken broth
Salt
Croutons

Force the avocado through a sieve or food mill. Sauté the onion slowly in the butter, then stir in the flour and cook over low heat, stirring, for 2 or 3 minutes. Gradually stir in the broth and cook, stirring, until thickened. Add the avocado and season to taste with salt. Pour into soup bowl and sprinkle with croutons. You will have about 2 cups.

Cream of Celery Soup

1 cup finely sliced celery with leaves
2 tablespoons chopped onion
1½ teaspoons butter
1½ teaspoons flour
1½ cups milk
Salt
Freshly ground pepper
Chopped parsley

Cook the celery and onion in ½ cup of water until tender. Melt the butter in a saucepan, blend in the flour and cook over low heat, stirring, for 2 or 3 minutes. Add the milk and cook, stirring, until thickened. Stir in the cooked celery, onion and the cooking liquid, adding more milk only if too thick. Heat gently, seasoning to taste with salt and pepper. Garnish with chopped parsley. You will have about 2 cups.

Chicken Soup

Add fine noodles to this soup, or use it as stock in other soups. It freezes well.

1½ pounds chicken necks and backs
Salt
5 whole peppercorns
1 small carrot, halved
1 small onion, sliced
Few parsley sprigs or celery tops
Few dill sprigs

Put the chicken in a saucepan and add cold water to cover. Bring to a boil, add about 1 teaspoon salt and the peppercorns, carrot, onion, parsley and dill. Cover, reduce the heat and simmer very slowly for 1½–2 hours. Strain, chill and skim off the fat. Add more salt to taste. You will have about 2 cups.

Chicken-Chutney Soup

A little chopped cooked chicken is a nice addition to this soup, if you happen to have some on hand.

1¼ cups seasoned chicken broth or Chicken Soup (p. 9)
¼ teaspoon curry powder
1 tablespoon chopped mango chutney
1 egg yolk
2 tablespoons heavy cream
¼ teaspoon lemon juice
2 tablespoons finely diced peeled cucumber
Toasted coconut (optional)

Combine the chicken broth, curry powder and chutney in a saucepan and bring to a boil; remove from the heat. Beat the egg yolk with the cream and gradually add to the broth, beating with a whisk. Add the lemon juice and chill well. Before eating, garnish with cucumber, and coconut if desired. You will have about 2 cups.

Eggdrop Soup

If you stir in the egg slowly, you will have large eggdrops; stir it in fast, and the eggdrops will be small.

2 cups seasoned chicken broth or Chicken Soup (p. 9)
1 egg
¼ teaspoon dry sherry
2 teaspoons minced green onion

Bring the broth to a boil in a saucepan. Beat the egg slightly with the sherry. Stir the egg mixture into the boiling soup, then remove from the heat. Pour into soup bowl and sprinkle with the green onion. You will have about 2 cups.

Spring Soup

1½ cups chicken broth or Chicken Soup (p. 9)
1 tablespoon thinly sliced green onion
¼ cup chopped watercress
½ cup cooked rice

Combine the broth and green onion in a saucepan and simmer for 5 minutes. Stir in the watercress and rice and simmer for 5 minutes more. You will have about 2 cups.

Sprout Soup

1½ cups seasoned chicken or beef broth
½ cup bean sprouts
1 egg, well beaten
1 tablespoon minced parsley

Heat the broth, then add the sprouts and simmer for 3 minutes. Remove from the heat and stir in the egg. Garnish with parsley. You will have about 2 cups.

Mushroom Soup

Perfect for a "soup and sandwich" meal.

¼ pound fresh mushrooms
2 cups chicken broth
1 tablespoon butter
1 tablespoon flour
¼ teaspoon salt
Freshly ground pepper
Pinch of ginger
¼ cup light cream or milk (optional)
Chopped parsley

Remove the stems from the mushrooms and chop the stems fine. Put the broth in a saucepan, add the mushroom stems, cover and simmer for 20 minutes. Slice the mushroom caps thin and sauté them in the butter for 2 or 3 minutes. Blend in the flour, salt, pepper and ginger and cook over low heat, stirring, for about 3 minutes. Gradually stir in the stock-and-mushroom mixture and cook over medium heat, stirring, until slightly thickened. Add cream if you wish, and sprinkle with parsley. You will have about 2 cups.

Onion Soup with Cheese Toast

Soup and sandwich in one bowl—a complete and nourishing dinner for one.

1½ tablespoons butter
½ pound onions, sliced thin
1½ tablespoons flour
2 cups beef broth
Salt
Freshly ground pepper
Chopped parsley
Cheese Toast (see below)

Melt the butter in a saucepan, add the onions and sauté over medium heat for about 10 minutes, or until the onions are golden but not brown. Blend in the flour and cook over low heat, stirring, for 2 or 3 minutes. Gradually stir in the broth and cook, stirring, until slightly thickened. Cover and simmer for about 30 minutes. Season to taste with salt and pepper and sprinkle with parsley. Serve in a bowl over Cheese Toast. You will have 2–2½ cups.

CHEESE TOAST
Toast *¾-inch slices of French or Italian bread.* Cover each slice of bread with a *¼-inch slice of Swiss cheese,* sprinkle with *freshly grated Parmesan cheese* and broil for 2 minutes or until the cheese is slightly melted.

Onion-Potato Soup

This soup is a winner, tasty and satisfying. Try it when you feel you need a little pampering.

1–2 tablespoons butter
1 small onion, sliced thin
1 medium potato, peeled and sliced thin
1 cup hot chicken broth
2 peppercorns, bruised
2 whole allspice, bruised
¼ cup finely chopped celery tops
2 tablespoons heavy cream (optional)
Salt
Freshly ground pepper

Melt the butter in a saucepan. Add the onion and potato and sauté, stirring, for 5 minutes. Stir in the chicken broth, peppercorns and allspice. Bring to a boil, cover and simmer for about 30 minutes, or until the potatoes are very tender. Beat the soup with a whisk until the potatoes are broken up into tiny little pieces. Add the celery tops, and the cream if desired. Heat and season to taste with salt and pepper. You will have about 2 cups.

Tomato and Green-Pepper Soup

Hearty enough to be a meal in itself, a cup of this perky soup also makes a fine beginning to a fish dinner.

1 large or 2 small tomatoes, peeled and diced
1 small green pepper, diced
1 leek, sliced thin
1½ cups chicken broth
2 teaspoons cornstarch
Salt
Freshly ground pepper
¼ teaspoon fresh thyme or generous pinch of dried thyme
1 tablespoon minced parsley
1 tablespoon minced chives

Combine the tomato, green pepper, leek and chicken broth in a saucepan. Bring to a boil, cover, reduce heat and simmer for 15 minutes. Mix the cornstarch with a little cold water until smooth, then stir it into the soup mixture. Bring to a boil, stirring, then simmer for a few minutes until slightly thickened. Season to taste with salt, pepper and thyme. When ready to eat, add the parsley and chives. You will have about 2 cups.

Escarole-Lentil Soup

Eat this with a crusty roll, a green salad and some cheese for a hearty, filling winter meal for one.

1 tablespoon oil
1 small onion, chopped
About 1½ cups chicken broth
½ cup lentils, rinsed
¼ pound escarole, in bite-sized pieces
Salt
Freshly ground pepper
Freshly grated Parmesan cheese

Heat the oil in a saucepan and sauté the onion in it for about 5 minutes, or until tender. Stir in the broth and the lentils. Bring to a boil, cover, reduce the heat, and simmer for 1 hour, or until the lentils are tender. Add the escarole, salt and pepper to taste, cover and cook for 10 minutes more, stirring occasionally. Add additional broth if the soup seems too thick. Sprinkle generously with Parmesan cheese before eating. You will have about 2 cups.

Lentil Soup with Vegetables

⅓ cup lentils, rinsed
2 slices bacon, in small pieces
2 teaspoons flour
½ cup beef broth
⅓ cup chopped leek or onion
2 teaspoons finely chopped green pepper
2 teaspoons finely chopped carrots
Salt
Cider vinegar (optional)

Put the lentils in a pot and cover with 2 cups of cold water. Bring to a boil, skim, cover and simmer for about 1 hour, or until the lentils are very soft. Force them through a sieve or food mill and set aside.

Sauté the bacon until crisp; remove. Heat 2 teaspoons of the bacon drippings over low heat. Blend in the flour and cook, stirring, for about 2 minutes. Gradually pour in the broth and cook, stirring, until smooth and thickened. Add the lentil purée, leek, green pepper and carrots. Bring to a boil, cover and simmer for about 30 minutes. Add the bacon and season to taste with salt, and vinegar if desired. Cook about 5 minutes more. You will have about 2 cups.

Creamy Carrot Soup

1 cup carrots, in ½-inch slices
1 cup chicken broth or Chicken Soup (p. 9)
1 whole green onion, in 2-inch pieces
½ cup nonfat dry-milk powder dissolved in ½ cup water
Salt
Freshly ground pepper
Minced green onion (optional)

Cook the carrots in the chicken broth for 10 to 15 minutes, or until tender. Put in a blender or food processor, add the green onion and purée until smooth. Return to the saucepan, stir in the milk and heat. Season to taste with salt and pepper. Eat hot or cold, sprinkled with minced green onion if you wish. You will have about 2 cups.

Zucchini Purée

Eat this soup immediately, garnished with thin slices of frankfurter, for a hot, winter meal. Eat it cold, garnished with sliced stuffed green olives, for a cool summer lunch. It's easy to prepare in advance, and nice to have on hand when you don't have time to cook.

½ onion, chopped
1 tablespoon butter
1 cup chicken broth
1 cup diced zucchini
Pinch of garlic powder
Pinch of celery salt
Salt
Freshly ground pepper
2 tablespoons parsley leaves

Sauté the onion in the butter in a saucepan until tender. Add the broth, zucchini, garlic powder, celery salt and some salt and pepper, and cook over medium heat for about 10–15 minutes, or until the zucchini is tender. Put in a blender, add the parsley and purée until smooth. Adjust the seasonings, and thin with more broth if you wish. You will have about 2 cups.

Cold Clam or Salmon Bisque

Accompanied by a light salad, this solitary summer lunch is most appealing.

1 can (about 7 ounces) chilled minced clams or salmon, undrained
1 cup half-and-half or light cream
Pinch of salt
Dash of hot-pepper sauce
Sprig of fresh dill or pinch of dried dillweed
Breadsticks or croutons

Put the clams or salmon, the half-and-half, salt, pepper sauce and dill in a food processor or blender. Purée until smooth. Eat chilled with breadsticks or croutons. You will have about 2 cups.

Cold Buttermilk Borsch

½ cup drained, canned beets, cut up
1 cup buttermilk
¼ cup creamed cottage cheese
1 teaspoon lemon juice
⅛ teaspoon salt

Put all the ingredients in a blender or food processor. Add ½ cup of crushed ice cubes and whirl for about 30 seconds. Garnish with a few shoestring beets if you wish, and eat immediately. You will have about 2 cups.

Chilled Yogurt-Cucumber Soup

Top your soup bowl with sliced cucumber, and chopped fresh dill if you have some.

1 large cucumber, peeled and sliced thin
¼ teaspoon salt
¾ teaspoon sugar
1 teaspoon olive oil
½ cup plain yogurt

Mix the cucumber, salt, sugar and olive oil together in a bowl. Fold in the yogurt and chill for at least 2 hours. Purée in a blender or food processor and eat chilled. You will have 1½–2 cups.

Gazpacho Andaluz

Garnish this cool, tangy, summery soup with little bits of chopped cucumber, pimiento or tomato.

1 clove garlic, minced
¾ teaspoon salt
Freshly ground pepper
½ teaspoon cumin seed
2 ripe tomatoes, quartered
½ small sweet red pepper, sliced
½ small cucumber, sliced
2 tablespoons oil
2 teaspoons vinegar
1 egg

Put the garlic, salt, pepper, cumin, tomatoes, red pepper and cucumber in the container of a blender or food processor. Purée until liquid, adding 1 tablespoon of water if necessary. Strain. Return to the blender and add the oil, vinegar and raw egg. Purée until smooth and blended. Pour into a bowl, stir in 1 cup of cold water and chill. You will have about 2 cups of gazpacho.

Iced Creamy Vegetable Soup

⅓ cup diced raw potato
2 tablespoons sliced green onion
⅓ cup raw peas, fresh or frozen
2 tablespoons sliced celery
½ cup chicken broth
⅓ cup light cream
Salt
Freshly ground pepper
Chopped chives

Put the potato, green onion, peas and celery in a sauce-pan, cover with the broth and cook, covered, until tender. Let cool. Purée until smooth in a blender or food processor. Add the cream and blend just long enough to mix. Season to taste with salt and pepper. Chill. Before eating, add more seasoning if necessary, and sprinkle bowl with chives. You will have about 2 cups.

Watercress Soup

Quick, cool and refreshing.

1 cup coarsely chopped watercress, including stems
¼ cup sour cream
8 ounces clam-tomato juice
Pinch of cayenne
¼ teaspoon salt
Sour cream (optional)

Put all the ingredients in a blender and whirl until smooth. Chill. Top the bowl with a dollop of sour cream if you wish. You will have about 2 cups.

SANDWICHES, HAMBURGERS and FRANKS

❀❀❀❀❀❀❀❀❀❀❀❀❀❀❀❀❀❀❀❀❀❀❀❀❀❀❀❀❀

ⓄⲎⓄⲎⓄⲎⓄⲎⓄⲎⓄⲎⓄⲎⓄⲎⓄⲎⓄⲎⓄⲎⓄⲎⓄⲎⓄⲎⓄⲎⓄⲎⓄⲎⓄⲎⓄⲎ

WHY PUT SANDWICHES, HAMBURGERS AND FRANKFURTERS up front in this book? Because we're practical and know that people who live alone often tend to "settle" for these snacks rather than preparing a full-course meal—especially when they're not in the mood to cook. There's usually something around for a sandwich, and hot dogs and hamburgers are easy to get and to fix. No one, after all, is waiting for a real dinner to be made; there's no one to disappoint but yourself.

But we also know how to avoid such disappointments. There are lots of ways to make sandwiches interesting and imaginative, and dozens of variations on hamburgers and hot dogs that will make them very special treats.

Roast Beef and Spicy Sour Cream Sandwich

2 tablespoons sour cream
1 teaspoon dry onion-soup mix
Freshly ground pepper
2 slices rye bread
Butter
3 slices cold roast beef
1 lettuce leaf
1 slice dill pickle (optional)

Mix the sour cream, onion-soup mix and pepper together. Spread the bread with butter. Place the roast beef on one of the bread slices. Top with the sour-cream mixture and the lettuce, and cover with the second slice of bread. Cut in half, and eat with a slice of dill pickle if you wish.

Barbecued Meat on a Bun

2 ounces beef broth
2 ounces tomato sauce or ketchup
1 tablespoon packed brown sugar
1½ teaspoons cider vinegar
1 teaspoon prepared mustard
Salt
Freshly ground pepper
½ cup diced cooked beef, pork or ham
1 sandwich bun, split
1 green onion, sliced

Mix the broth, tomato sauce, brown sugar, vinegar, mustard, salt and pepper together in a small saucepan. Cook over medium heat, stirring occasionally, until the sauce is thickened and well blended, about 20–25 minutes. Stir in the meat and heat. Open the bun on a plate, sprinkle it with the green onion and spoon the hot meat mixture over it. Eat at once.

Broiled Meat-Tomato-Cheese Sandwich

2 tablespoons mayonnaise
¼ teaspoon prepared mustard
1 or 2 slices bread, lightly toasted
2 thin slices cooked ham, chicken, turkey or tongue
2 slices tomato
Salt
Freshly ground pepper
2 tablespoons coarsely shredded Muenster, Cheddar or
    Swiss cheese

Blend the mayonnaise and mustard together and spread some of it thinly on 1 slice of toast. Top with 2 meat slices and then with 2 tomato slices. Season with salt and pepper. Stir the cheese into the remaining mayonnaise mixture and spoon it onto the tomatoes. Broil about 4 inches from the heat until the cheese is bubbly and lightly browned, about 2 minutes. Eat at once, either open-faced or topped with another piece of toast.

French-Toasted Bologna-Cheese Sandwich

Try this with ham, too.

2 slices white bread
Mustard
2 slices bologna
1 slice American cheese
1 egg
2–3 tablespoons milk
Butter
Celery stick (optional)

Spread the bread with mustard and make a bologna-cheese sandwich. Beat the egg and milk together in a shallow bowl. Dip the sandwich in the egg mixture, turning carefully with a spatula, until all of it is absorbed. Melt a little butter in a skillet and toast the sandwich in it on both sides, turning with a spatula and adding more butter if necessary. Cut in half and eat immediately, garnished with a celery stick if desired.

Cheese Fondue Sandwich

1 small slice firm French or Italian bread
¼ pound diced sharp Cheddar cheese
¼ cup milk
¼ teaspoon dry mustard
Salt
Dash of cayenne
1 teaspoon butter
2 slices toast
Paprika

Cut the crust from the bread and cut it into ¼-inch cubes. Put the cubes in the top of a double boiler and add the cheese, milk, mustard, salt and cayenne. Cook over simmering water, stirring constantly, until the cheese melts and the mixture thickens. Beat in the butter and cook 3 minutes more. Serve over toast with a sprinkling of paprika.

Cheese Rabbit

½ cup diced sharp Cheddar cheese
1½ teaspoons flour
¼ teaspoon dry mustard
⅛ teaspoon salt
1 teaspoon butter
3 tablespoons hot milk
1 English muffin, split and toasted

Put all the ingredients except the English muffin in a blender and whirl until smooth. Heat in a double boiler over simmering water. Serve over the English muffin.

Thin-Boy Sandwich

Hearty, healthy eating.

1 long French roll, split lengthwise
Mayonnaise
3 ounces cottage cheese
½ small cucumber, peeled and sliced
French dressing
Salt
Freshly ground pepper
1 small tomato, sliced
3 radishes, sliced
3 green onions, sliced
1 slice sharp Cheddar cheese
Lettuce or other salad green

Spread each half of the French roll with mayonnaise. Pile half the cottage cheese on the bottom half of the roll. Arrange the cucumber slices on top of the cottage cheese. Drizzle with a little French dressing and dust with salt and pepper. Add the remaining cottage cheese, then add the tomato, radishes, onions and Cheddar cheese, sprinkling each with a little dressing and the seasonings. Add the lettuce and the top of the roll.

Broiled Cheese-Topped Chicken Sandwich

1 crusty roll, split
Mayonnaise
Thyme
2 ounces sliced cooked chicken
¼ cup shredded Muenster cheese

Spread both halves of the roll liberally with mayonnaise and sprinkle lightly with thyme. Broil the bottom half for 1 or 2 minutes until the mayonnaise bubbles. Arrange the chicken on the broiled bottom half. Mix the cheese with 1 tablespoon of mayonnaise and spread it on the chicken. Place the top half alongside the bottom half and broil both for 2 or 3 minutes until the cheese is bubbly and hot. Close the sandwich and eat immediately.

Chicken Club Sandwich

The asparagus, bacon and sliced egg make this very special.

3 slices white bread or toast
Softened butter
1 lettuce leaf
4 fresh cold cooked or canned asparagus tips
1 large slice cold cooked chicken breast
Mayonnaise
4 slices crisp bacon
1 cold hard-cooked egg, sliced

Spread one side of each slice of bread with butter. Arrange the lettuce, asparagus and chicken on one buttered slice. Cover with another slice, buttered side down. Spread the top side with mayonnaise, then cover with the bacon and egg slices. Close the sandwich with remaining slice of bread, buttered side down. Cut in quarters.

Eggburger

1 seeded roll
1 thin slice American cheese
1 egg
Butter
Salt
Freshly ground pepper
1 thin onion slice
Chili sauce, chopped-pickle relish or mustard

Split the roll and toast it. Put the cheese on the top half. Fry the egg in a little butter, turning it once. Place on bottom half of roll, sprinkle with salt and pepper, and top with the onion slice. Add whatever relishes you wish, put the two halves together and eat at once.

Swiss Omelet Sandwich

1 egg, beaten
1 link sausage, cooked and sliced thin
3 mushrooms, sliced
1 teaspoon chopped green pepper
Salt
Freshly ground pepper
Softened butter
2 slices pumpernickel, toasted
1 slice Swiss cheese

Mix the egg, sausage, mushrooms, green pepper, salt and pepper together; set aside. Spread the toast with butter, cover 1 slice with the cheese and put it under the broiler.

While the cheese melts, heat some butter in a small skillet, pour in the egg mixture and make an omelet, cooking until the top is set but still moist and the bottom lightly browned. Fold the omelet and put it on the second piece of toast, cover it with the melted-cheese toast and eat at once.

Broiled Egg-Salad Sandwich

1 hard-cooked egg, coarsely chopped
About 1 tablespoon mayonnaise
1 tablespoon chopped celery
2 teaspoons chopped onion
About ¼ teaspoon prepared mustard
Salt
Freshly ground pepper
2 slices bread
2 thin slices cooked ham or bologna

Combine the egg, mayonnaise, celery, onion, mustard, salt and pepper. Toast both sides of the bread under the broiler. Cover each slice with a slice of ham, then spread each with some egg salad. Return to the broiler and broil until golden brown.

Chopped-Chicken-Liver Sandwich

Pickled beets go well with chicken-liver sandwiches.

2 ounces (about ¼ cup) chicken livers
1 tablespoon chicken fat or oil
½ small onion, minced
1 hard-cooked egg
Salt
Freshly ground pepper
1 bagel, split, toasted and buttered, or 2 slices
    pumpernickel
Lettuce leaf

Sauté the chicken livers in the fat until they are lightly browned. Add the onion and cook until it is tender and the livers are cooked through. Remove the livers and onion with pan juices to a chopping board, add the egg and chop or mash until fine. Season to taste with salt and pepper. Spread on half the bagel, add the lettuce and close the sandwich.

Hot Mushroom Sandwich

3 ounces mushrooms, chopped fine
1 teaspoon minced onion
Butter
Salt
Freshly ground pepper
2 teaspoons chopped dill pickle
1 teaspoon mayonnaise
2 thin slices white bread

Sauté the mushrooms and onion in butter until lightly browned. Add the salt, pepper, pickle and mayonnaise, adjusting the seasonings to your taste. Brush both sides of the bread with melted butter. Spread the mushroom filling on one slice of bread, cover with the other, then cut the sandwich in thirds. Toast both sides under the broiler and eat at once.

Tuna Sandwich Roll

Use the tuna that is left over from this recipe to make
Tuna Mayonnaise (p. 201).

About 2½ ounces tuna, drained and flaked
About 2 tablespoons mayonnaise
2 tablespoons diced celery
1 teaspoon minced green onion
½ teaspoon prepared mustard
Softened butter
1 sandwich roll, split

Mix the tuna, mayonnaise, celery, green onion and mustard to taste. Butter the sandwich roll and fill it with the
tuna mixture.

Broiled Tuna-Cheese Sandwich

Eat this open-faced, or add another slice of toast, if you
wish, for a closed sandwich.

About 2½ ounces tuna, drained and flaked
2 tablespoons finely chopped celery
About 2 tablespoons mayonnaise
Salt
Freshly ground pepper
Squeeze of lemon juice
Dash of hot-pepper sauce
1 slice white or whole-wheat bread, toasted
2 tablespoons shredded Cheddar cheese

Mix together the tuna, celery, mayonnaise, salt, pepper, lemon juice and pepper sauce. Toast the bread lightly and spread with the tuna mixture. Sprinkle with the cheese and broil until the cheese has melted. Eat at once.

Tuna-Cream Cheese Sandwich

This elegant presentation of a tuna sandwich will make you feel very special.

1½ ounces cream cheese
1 teaspoon lemon juice
About 2 tablespoons mayonnaise
About 1½ tablespoons chopped green olives
2½–3 ounces tuna, drained and flaked
Salt
Freshly ground pepper
2 slices white bread
1 slice whole-wheat bread
Softened butter
3 tablespoons coarsely chopped salted pecans

Blend the cream cheese, lemon juice and mayonnaise until smooth, then fold in the olives and tuna. Season to taste with salt and pepper. Trim the crusts off the bread and butter each slice. Spread 1 slice of white bread with ⅓ of the tuna mixture, then cover with the whole-wheat bread. On it, spread about another ⅓ of the tuna mixture, and top with the white bread. Cut the sandwich into 4 triangles. Spread the remaining tuna mixture on the edges of each triangle. Dip each edge in the chopped pecans.

Walnut-Tuna Sandwich

2½ ounces tuna, drained and flaked
2 tablespoons finely chopped walnuts
Squeeze of lemon juice
About 2 tablespoons mayonnaise
Salt
Pepper
2 slices rye bread
Softened butter

Mix the tuna, walnuts and lemon juice with enough mayonnaise to moisten. Season to taste with salt and pepper. Spread the rye bread with butter and fill with the tuna mixture.

Meat Tacos

Fill each taco with shredded lettuce and some shredded Cheddar cheese and eat with canned pinto beans, if you wish to transform this simple dish into a Mexican feast for one.

½ small onion, chopped
1 teaspoon oil
¼ pound ground beef
½ small clove garlic, minced
⅓ cup tomato sauce
Salt
Pinch of oregano
Pinch of crushed red pepper
2 taco shells

Sauté the onion in oil until it is tender. Add the meat and garlic, and cook, stirring, until lightly browned; drain off any excess fat. Add the tomato sauce, salt, oregano and red pepper, and cook, stirring occasionally, for about 5 minutes. Taste and adjust the seasonings. Spoon into warm tacos and eat immediately.

Tuna Tacos

This uncooked taco filling makes an easy lunch or light summer dinner for one.

1 can (3½ ounces) tuna, drained
2 tablespoons mayonnaise
2 tablespoons chopped green onion or celery
1½ tablespoons chili sauce
Salt
Freshly ground pepper
2 taco shells
Shredded lettuce
Shredded Cheddar cheese
½ small tomato, cut in small pieces

Mix the tuna, mayonnaise, onion, chili sauce, salt and pepper. Spoon into the taco shells and top with the lettuce, cheese and tomato.

Piquant Hamburger

¼ pound ground beef
Salt
Freshly ground pepper
Pinch of crushed marjoram leaves
1 green onion, sliced thin
2 teaspoons chopped parsley
¼ teaspoon relish
2 teaspoons drained capers
1 tablespoon red wine or broth
1 split, toasted hamburger bun

Lightly mix all the ingredients and shape into a patty. Broil or pan-fry until done as you like it, allowing about 4 or 5 minutes on each side for medium. Put in the hamburger bun and eat at once.

Blue-Cheese and Bacon Burger

2 teaspoons soft butter
2 teaspoons chopped parsley
2 teaspoons chopped green onion
1 hamburger bun, split
¼ pound ground beef
2 tablespoons crumbled blue cheese
1 slice bacon, halved

Combine the butter, parsley and green onion. Spread on both halves of the hamburger bun and toast under the broiler. Combine the beef and cheese and shape into a patty. Broil on one side for about 5–8 minutes, or until almost done. Turn, top with bacon and broil for 4 or 5 minutes, or until the bacon is crisp. Put in the bun and eat at once.

Savory Hamburger

¼ pound ground beef
1½ tablespoons sour cream
2 teaspoons bread crumbs
2–3 chopped mushrooms, sautéed in a little butter
1 green onion, sliced fine
2 teaspoons chopped parsley
¼ teaspoon salt
Freshly ground pepper
1 split, toasted hamburger bun

Lightly mix all the hamburger ingredients together and shape into a patty. Broil or pan-fry to the desired degree of doneness, allowing about 4 or 5 minutes on each side for medium. Put the hamburger in the bun and eat at once.

Stuffed Hamburger

A nice way to "stretch" a hamburger when you're feeling especially hungry.

¼ pound ground beef
1 slice tomato
Diced American cheese
1 green onion, sliced thin
Dill-pickle slices
1 toasted, buttered, split hamburger bun

Divide the meat and shape into 2 thin patties. Put the tomato, cheese, onion and pickle slices between the patties, press the edges together and broil or pan-fry until done as you like it, allowing about 4 to 5 minutes on each side for medium. Lift with a spatula into the hamburger bun and eat immediately.

Double-Decker Burger

¼ pound ground lean beef
1 tablespoon Russian Dressing (p. 200)
1 hamburger bun, split and toasted
Pickle slices
1 tablespoon chopped onion
¼ cup shredded lettuce
1 slice American cheese

Divide the beef in half and shape into 2 thin patties. Broil or pan-fry them to the desired degree of doneness, allowing about 4 or 5 minutes on each side for medium. Spoon the dressing onto the bottom of the bun, top with a patty, then add the pickle slices, onion and lettuce. Add the remaining patty, cheese and the top of the bun. Eat at once.

Cheese-Walnut Burger

¼ pound ground lean beef
1 teaspoon red wine
½ teaspoon Worcestershire sauce
¼ teaspoon salt
⅛ teaspoon Dijon-style mustard
Freshly ground pepper
1 ounce (about ¼ cup) shredded Cheddar cheese
1½ tablespoons chopped walnuts
1 split, toasted hamburger bun

Combine all the hamburger ingredients, mixing them thoroughly but lightly. Shape into a patty and grill it under the broiler for about 4 or 5 minutes on each side, or until done to your preference. Put in the bun and eat at once.

Dillburger

¼ teaspoon crushed dill seed
1 tablespoon chopped green olives or sweet pickles
¼ pound ground beef
Salt
Freshly ground pepper
1 split, toasted hamburger bun

Mix the dill seed, olives and meat together lightly, season
to taste with salt and pepper and shape into a patty. Broil
or pan-fry until done as you like it, allowing about 4 or 5
minutes on each side for medium. Put in the bun and eat
at once.

Sesame Burger

1–2 tablespoons sesame seed
¼ pound ground beef
Salt
Freshly ground pepper
2 slices buttered toast

Preheat the oven to 350°.
Toast the sesame seed for about 10 minutes, or until
lightly browned. Add to the ground beef, season to taste
with salt and pepper and shape into a patty. Broil or
pan-fry until cooked to your preference, allowing about
4 or 5 minutes on each side for medium. Put between the
slices of toast and eat at once.

Cheeseburger de Luxe

¼ pound ground beef
⅓ cup shredded sharp Cheddar cheese
1½ teaspoons grated onion
1 teaspoon steak sauce
Freshly ground pepper
1 slice bacon, partially cooked
Slice of hot buttered French bread or toast
2 teaspoons soft butter
1 teaspoon minced green olives

Mix the beef, cheese, onion, steak sauce and pepper together lightly and shape into a patty. Wrap the bacon around it and secure it with a toothpick. Sauté until done as you like it, allowing about 4 or 5 minutes on each side for medium. Place on bread and dot with a mixture of the butter and the olives.

Deep-Fried Hamburger Sandwich

The meat in this deep-fried burger will be rare. If you prefer it more well-done, cook it first.

¼ pound ground beef
2 slices fresh bread, crusts removed
Salt
Freshly ground pepper
1 egg, beaten
¼ cup milk
Fat for deep-frying

Shape the meat into a patty and put in the center of one of the bread slices. Sprinkle with salt and pepper and top with the other slice of bread. Press the edges of the 2 slices of bread together with your fingers, then seal them with the tines of a fork dipped in hot water. Mix the egg and the milk. Dip the sandwich in the mixture, then fry it in hot deep fat (375° on a frying thermometer) until golden brown. Drain on a paper towel, then eat at once.

Steak Tartare Sandwich

Easy and elegant, this is also very special grilled over charcoal.

¼ pound very lean ground beef
¼ teaspoon salt
Freshly ground pepper
2 slices white bread

Lightly toss the beef with the salt and pepper. Spread on 1 slice of unbuttered bread, then top with the other slice. Toast under the broiler until bread is golden brown, allowing a minute or two for each side.

Hamburger with Pepper and Onion

¼ pound ground beef
Salt
Freshly ground pepper
½ onion, sliced thin
½ green pepper, sliced thin
2 teaspoons vegetable oil

Season the meat with salt and pepper, shape into a patty and broil or pan-fry until done as you like it, allowing 4 or 5 minutes on each side for medium. While the hamburger is cooking, sauté the onion in hot oil until golden. Add the green pepper and cook until the pepper is crisp-tender. Season to taste with salt and pepper and spoon over the hamburger before you eat it. You can also eat this in a roll if you wish.

Hawaiian Hamburger

¼ pound ground lean beef
½ small onion, minced
½ small clove garlic, minced
2 tablespoons soy sauce
Pinch of ground ginger

Mix the beef and onion and shape into 1 or 2 patties. Put in a small bowl. Mix the garlic, soy sauce and ginger and pour over the patty or patties. Let stand for 30 minutes, turning once. Drain, then broil or pan-fry, allowing about 4 or 5 minutes on each side for medium. Eat with spiced fruit if you wish.

Hamburger with Filberts

¼ pound ground beef
Salt
Freshly ground pepper
¼ cup chopped filberts
Butter

Mix the beef lightly with salt, pepper and half the filberts. Shape into a patty and broil until done as you like it, allowing 4 or 5 minutes on each side for medium. Sprinkle the remaining filberts over the top, dot with butter and return to the broiler for just a few seconds to brown the nuts. Spoon the drippings over the burger and eat at once.

Peppy Hamburger Steak

¼ pound ground beef
2–3 tablespoons soft bread crumbs
2 tablespoons milk or evaporated milk
¼ teaspoon salt
Freshly ground pepper
Dash of Worcestershire sauce
1 thick slice onion
1 green-pepper ring
⅓ cup tomato juice
1½ tablespoons ketchup
1 teaspoon prepared mustard

Mix the beef, bread crumbs, milk, salt and pepper and shape into one thick patty. Brown on both sides in a greased skillet. Pour off any fat. Add a dash of Worcestershire sauce to the patty, then top with the onion and green pepper. Mix the tomato juice, ketchup and mustard and pour over the patty. Bring to a boil, cover and simmer for about 15 minutes.

Teriyaki Burger

¼ pound ground beef
1 green onion, sliced fine
1 tablespoon finely chopped green pepper
1 tablespoon chopped water chestnuts
1 teaspoon soy sauce
1 teaspoon lemon juice
2 teaspoons water
1 teaspoon brown sugar
Generous pinch of ground ginger

BASTING SAUCE:
1 teaspoon brown sugar }
1 teaspoon soy sauce   } mixed together

Mix together lightly all the ingredients except those for
the basting sauce. Shape into a patty and broil or pan-fry
until done as you like it, allowing 4 or 5 minutes on each
side for medium. Just before the hamburger is done,
brush it with the basting sauce and cook it a few seconds
longer.

Chinese-Style Hamburger

¼ pound ground beef
Salt
Freshly ground pepper
1 tablespoon butter
1½ teaspoons soy sauce
¼ teaspoon molasses
¾ cup bean sprouts, drained
1 pimiento, cut up

Season the meat wtih salt and pepper and shape it into a patty. Broil or pan-fry until done as you like it, allowing about 4 or 5 minutes on each side for medium. While the hamburger is cooking, melt the butter in a small skillet and stir in the soy sauce and molasses. Add the beans sprouts, toss and heat. Add the pimiento. Spoon over the hamburger before you eat it.

Bean-Sprout Burger

Keep any leftover bean sprouts in the refrigerator and use them in salads and soups. Put drained, leftover water chestnuts in a jar filled with cold water and a teaspoon or two of salt; packed that way and refrigerated, they will keep for many months.

¼ pound ground beef
2–3 tablespoons bean sprouts
1 tablespoon chopped water chestnuts
1½ teaspoons soy sauce
1½ tablespoons sliced green onion
1 teaspoon oil
1 tablespoon mayonnaise
½ teaspoon lemon juice
⅛ teaspoon prepared mustard

Mix the beef, bean sprouts, water chestnuts, soy sauce and 1 tablespoon of the green onion. Shape into a patty and fry in the oil until cooked to your preference. Mix the mayonnaise, lemon juice and mustard. Spoon over the burger and sprinkle with the remaining green onion.

Salisbury Steak with Mushroom Sauce

¼ pound ground lean beef
¼ teaspoon salt
Freshly ground pepper
6–8 mushrooms, chopped
1 tablespoon butter
1 tablespoon flour
½ teaspoon curry powder
½ cup beef bouillon

Mix the meat with salt and pepper, and shape into a patty. Pan-fry in a lightly greased skillet until cooked to your preference, allowing about 4 or 5 minutes on each side for medium; remove and keep warm. Cook the mushrooms in the butter for 2 or 3 minutes. Blend in the flour and curry powder, and cook for another 2 or 3 minutes, stirring. Add the beef bouillon and cook, stirring frequently, until smooth and thickened. Pour over the meat patty and eat at once.

North American Chili

This simple dish is made with lima beans instead of the traditional pinto beans, but any beans you may have available in small quantity will be fine here.

½ small onion, chopped
¼ pound ground lean beef
¾ teaspoon chili powder, or to taste
¼ teaspoon salt
½ can (about 4 ounces) lima beans, drained
1 can (8 ounces) tomatoes

Cook the onion and the beef in a skillet, breaking up the meat with a fork and stirring until it loses its red color. Add the chili powder, salt, lima beans and tomatoes, bring to a boil, cover and simmer for about 20 minutes, stirring occasionally. Taste and adjust seasonings before sitting down to eat.

Chili Porcupine Balls

Double this recipe if you wish: chili balls improve with age and may be reheated several days later for another meal. They also freeze well.

¼ pound ground beef
2 tablespoons uncooked rice
½ small onion, chopped
¼ teaspoon salt
Freshly ground pepper
1 tablespoon butter
1 can (8 ounces) tomato sauce
¼ cup water
¼ teaspoon chili powder, or to taste
Pinch of ground cumin

Mix the beef, rice, onion, salt and pepper. Shape into 5 or 6 small balls and brown them lightly on all sides in hot butter. Add the tomato sauce, water, chili powder and cumin, bring to the boil, cover and simmer for about 30 minutes.

Hamburger Stroganoff

¼ pound ground lean beef
1 tablespoon soft bread crumbs
½ small clove garlic, minced
2 tablespoons cold water
½ small onion, sliced
6–8 small mushrooms
1½ tablespoons vegetable oil
1 tablespoon flour
1 cup beef bouillon
1 teaspoon sherry
1 teaspoon tomato paste
Pinch of dry mustard
2–3 tablespoons sour cream

Mix the beef, bread crumbs, garlic and water, and shape into 1-inch balls. Cook the onion and mushrooms in 1 tablespoon of the oil for 5 minutes; remove from the pan and set aside. Pour the remaining ½ tablespoon of oil into the pan and brown the meatballs on all sides; remove the meatballs.

Blend in the flour in the skillet and brown it, stirring. Add the bouillon, sherry, tomato paste and mustard, and cook, stirring, until smooth and thickened. Add the meatballs, onion and mushrooms and simmer, uncovered, for about 15 minutes. Stir in the sour cream just before eating.

Peanut Hamburger Balls

These meatballs are good with spaghetti or noodles.

¼ pound ground lean beef
¼ cup crunchy peanut butter
½ small onion, minced
1 tablespoon chili sauce
¼ teaspoon salt
Freshly ground pepper
1 tablespoon cold water
1 tablespoon butter or oil
1 can (8 ounces) tomato sauce

Mix the beef, peanut butter, onion, chili sauce, salt, pepper and water. Shape into 1-inch balls. Brown in hot butter or oil, then pour off the fat. Cover the meatballs with tomato sauce and simmer, covered, for about 30 minutes. You will have enough extra sauce for spaghetti or noodles.

Frankfurters with Relish

2 frankfurters
Prepared mustard
Pickle relish
2 frankfurter rolls

Split the frankfurters lengthwise, halfway through. Spread the slit with mustard, fill it with relish and broil until sizzling. Eat in toasted rolls.

Frankfurters in Blankets

2 frankfurters
Pickle relish
2 slices fresh bread, crusts removed
2 slices bacon

Preheat the oven to 400°.

Split the frankfurters lengthwise, halfway through, and fill them with pickle relish. Wrap a slice of bread around each frankfurter. Roll a slice of bacon around each slice of bread. Secure with toothpicks if necessary. Put on a baking sheet and bake for about 15 minutes, until the bacon is crisp.

Cheese-Topped Frankfurters in Rolls

2 frankfurter rolls, split
Prepared mustard
1½ tablespoons soft butter
⅓ cup shredded sharp Cheddar cheese
1 egg white, beaten stiff
2 frankfurters

Preheat the oven to 425°.

Spread the insides of the frankfurter rolls with mustard. Cream the butter and cheese together until well blended; fold in the egg white. Split the frankfurter lengthwise almost all the way through. Put a frankfurter in each roll and top with the cheese mixture. Bake for about 15 minutes.

Frankfurters with Pepper and Onion

½ green pepper, sliced
1 small rib celery, sliced thin
½ onion, sliced
1 tablespoon oil
Salt
Freshly ground pepper
2 frankfurters, slit lengthwise
Prepared mustard
2 frankfurter rolls, split
Butter
2 teaspoons sesame seed

Sauté the pepper, celery and onion in hot oil until tender. Season with salt and pepper and set aside. Spread the frankfurters with mustard and broil until browned. Spread the cut sides of the rolls with butter and sprinkle with sesame seed. Toast under the broiler. Put a frankfurter in each roll and top with the pepper mixture.

Beer-Simmered Frankfurters

Eat these with sauerkraut and beans.

2 frankfurters
½ cup beer
2 peppercorns, bruised
½ bay leaf
1 frankfurter roll, split
Prepared mustard (optional)
Relish (optional)

Simmer the frankfurters, beer, peppercorns and bay leaf in an uncovered skillet for 5–10 minutes, until the frankfurters are heated through. Toast the roll and arrange it opened on a plate with the 2 frankfurters on it. Spread with mustard and relish if you wish.

Garlic-Pickled Frankfurters

Let these marinate overnight or during the day while you are at work.

¼ cup vinegar
¼ cup water
½ clove garlic
1 teaspoon whole mixed pickling spice
½ teaspoon sugar
2 frankfurters
2 teaspoons butter

Put the vinegar, water, garlic, pickling spice and sugar in a small pot and heat to the boiling point. Put the frankfurters in a small shallow dish and pour the vinegar mixture over them. Cover and refrigerate overnight. When ready to eat, remove the frankfurters from the marinade and sauté them in the butter until lightly browned.

Crusty Corn Dogs

Save the leftover egg to use in French toast or in your morning omelet.

3 tablespoons flour
1 tablespoon cornmeal
Generous pinch of salt
Generous pinch of baking soda
2 tablespoons buttermilk
1 egg, beaten
2 frankfurters
Oil for deep-frying
Prepared mustard

Mix 2 tablespoons of the flour with the cornmeal, salt and soda. Beat together the buttermilk and about ⅓ of the egg, then stir into the flour mixture until smooth. Cut the frankfurters in half crosswise, then roll in the rest of the flour to coat. Dip in the cornmeal batter until well coated. Fry in about 2 inches of hot oil (370° on a frying thermometer) for 2 or 3 minutes, or until golden brown. Drain on paper towels and eat hot with mustard.

Skillet Frankfurters and Beans

Easy to prepare and only one pot to wash.

2 frankfurters, sliced
2 teaspoons minced onion
½ clove garlic, minced
Pinch of oregano
2 teaspoons butter
1 can (8 ounces) baked beans
1 fresh tomato, in wedges

Sauté the frankfurters, onion, garlic and oregano in the hot butter until the franks are lightly browned. Add the beans and heat well. Add the tomato wedges and heat gently.

Frankfurter and Sauerkraut Goulash

You can make this ahead of time and reheat it if you wish.

2 frankfurters, sliced
2 tablespoons chopped onion
2 teaspoons butter
1 can (7¾ ounces) sauerkraut
¼ cup sour cream
1 teaspoon caraway seed
Salt
Paprika

Cook the frankfurters and onion in hot butter for about 5 minutes, stirring. Drain the sauerkraut, rinse it in cold water and drain again. Add it to the frankfurters and cook, covered, for 15 minutes. Add the sour cream, caraway seed, salt and paprika. Cook, uncovered, over low heat for about 5 minutes.

MEAT

❀)

⊙⫯

BEEF, VEAL, LAMB, PORK—each of these meats is available in cuts that are small enough for one serving, as you will see from the recipes in this chapter. If you usually buy meat for one, it's good to get to know your butcher, who can provide you with exactly the size and cut of meat that you wish. And if you're a steady customer, he won't mind the fact that your purchases are small. Supermarket meat packages almost always contain more than one person can use, and although most supermarkets will divide a package if you ask them to, it sometimes seems like a lot of bother.

Chops and steaks will keep in the refrigerator for two or three days. If you have more than you need, you can prepare them on different days in different ways. Or cook the meat all at one time and use what's left over in a dish that calls for cooked meat.

Roasts—even small roasts—are not for the single diner. Unless, of course, you have lots of empty freezer space and don't mind cooking a roast and then packaging the remainder in countless small parcels for future meals. It seems more practical to save roasts as a special company treat and use smaller cuts on a day-to-day basis.

Minute Steak au Poivre

Minute steaks are thin steaks cut from the ribs, the strip or the sirloin. They cook very quickly, but not really in a minute.

About 1–1½ teaspoons peppercorns
1 8-ounce minute steak
Butter
Salt

Crush the peppercorns in a mortar or with a mallet, keeping the pieces coarse. Press the crushed pepper firmly into both sides of the steak with the heel of your hand. Let stand for about 15 minutes. Cook the steak in a little butter in a skillet, allowing just a minute or so for each side. Dot with butter and sprinkle with salt before eating.

Club Steak with Onions

Steak smothered with onions is a great American favorite.

2 large sweet onions, peeled and sliced
Butter
Salt
Freshly ground pepper
1 club steak

Cook the onions very slowly in lots of butter in a covered skillet, stirring occasionally, until the onions are golden and flecked with brown. Season with salt and pepper. Pan-fry the steak in the same pan, pushing the onions aside, or broil it to the desired degree of doneness. Put the steak on a plate and cover it with the onions.

Charcoal-Broiled Tournedos

This dish is rich and extravagant: make it when you want a special treat. Charcoal grilling gives any steak a very special flavor, of course, but this will be fine broiled in the oven, too.

1 small filet mignon steak, about 1½ inches thick
Salt
Pepper
Béarnaise Sauce (p. 194)

Grill the steak over a medium charcoal fire or under the oven broiler, allowing 5 minutes for each side if you want it rare, 7–8 minutes if you like it medium. Sprinkle with salt and pepper. Serve with Béarnaise sauce.

Steak Kabobs

Set these to marinate a day ahead or before you leave home in the morning, and they will be ready to grill when you return at the end of the day.

½ pound boneless round steak, about 1 inch thick
1 small onion, sliced
2 tablespoons red wine or wine vinegar
2 tablespoons vegetable oil
Pinch of pepper
¼ teaspoon basil
Salt

Trim the meat and cut it in 1-inch cubes. Combine the rest of the ingredients in a mixing bowl. Add the meat, cover and refrigerate for about 12 hours.

When ready to grill, remove the meat from the marinade, reserving the marinade. Thread the meat on skewers and arrange on a broiler pan. Broil about 4 inches from the heat, basting with the marinade and turning the skewers occasionally, until brown, for about 8–10 minutes.

Beef in Burgundy

Prepare this dish well in advance; it improves with age.

¼–½ pound beef round, in julienne strips
1 tablespoon oil
¼ cup thinly sliced carrots
1–2 green onions, sliced
6 mushrooms, sliced thin
1 teaspoon flour
Salt
Freshly ground pepper
Pinch of thyme
3 tablespoons Burgundy
3 tablespoons beef broth

Brown the meat in the oil in a skillet. Remove the meat and reserve. Sauté the carrots and green onions in the pan drippings until the carrots are crisp-tender. Add the mushrooms and sauté 2 minutes more. Stir in the flour, salt, pepper and thyme, then gradually stir in the wine and broth. Return the meat to the pan, cover and simmer for 20 minutes, or until the meat is tender. Eat with rice or noodles if you wish.

Beef Juk

If you can't buy a very small piece of flank steak, slice the extra meat in strips and freeze them for future use. Flank steak can also be broiled or pan-fried in one piece, then sliced against the grain in thin diagonal slices.

2 tablespoons sesame seed
2 tablespoons soy sauce
2 teaspoons sugar
2 tablespoons oil
½ clove garlic, minced
Freshly ground pepper
¼–½ pound flank steak, in strips
3–4 green onions, in 2-inch pieces
Flour
1 egg, beaten

Combine the sesame seed, soy sauce, sugar, 2 teaspoons of the oil, garlic and pepper in a bowl. Add the meat and green onions, stir and let stand for 15 minutes. Remove the meat and onions to a piece of waxed paper and sprinkle them with a little flour. Heat a tablespoon or so of oil in a skillet, dip the meat and onions in the beaten egg, then fry in the hot oil until tender.

Beef Liver Orientale

¼ cup sliced green onions
2 tablespoons chopped celery
½ small clove garlic, crushed
1 tablespoon oil
½ pound beef liver, in 3-inch pieces
1 tablespoon flour
Pinch of ginger
Freshly ground pepper
1½ tablespoons soy sauce
1½ tablespoons water

Sauté the onions, celery and garlic in the oil until tender. Sprinkle the liver with half the flour. Push the vegetables to the side of the skillet and brown the liver, cooking 1 minute on each side. Remove the liver and set aside. Sprinkle the remaining flour, ginger and pepper over the vegetables, then stir in the soy sauce and water. Add the liver and cook, stirring, until the sauce thickens.

Veal Piccata

Tender, subtly flavored milk-fed veal is a delicacy these days, especially for those who have many mouths to feed. When you're dining alone, however, you can afford this lovely indulgence.

½ pound veal scaloppine
2 tablespoons flour
¼ teaspoon salt
Freshly ground pepper
1½ tablespoons butter
3 tablespoons freshly squeezed lemon juice
1 tablespoon water
1½ tablespoons chopped parsley
2 thin slices lemon

Pound the veal very thin with a wooden mallet or a rolling pin. Mix the flour, salt and pepper together and dredge the veal in the mixture. In a skillet, brown on both sides in the hot butter. Add the lemon juice, water and parsley and cook for 1 minute, scraping up the brown bits from the bottom of the pan. Put the meat on a plate, pour the sauce over it and garnish with the lemon slices.

Veal Scaloppine with Mushrooms

½ pound veal scaloppine
1½ tablespoons flour
¼ teaspoon salt
Freshly ground pepper
2 tablespoons butter
1 tablespoon dry Marsala or sherry
6–8 mushrooms, sliced
⅓ cup beef bouillon

Pound the veal very thin with a wooden mallet or a rolling pin. Mix the flour, salt and pepper together, coat the veal with the mixture and brown on both sides in hot butter. Add the wine and mushrooms and cook over moderately high heat for another 5 minutes or so, scraping the brown bits from the bottom of the pan. Remove the meat to a plate. Add the bouillon to the skillet, stir well, bring to a boil and pour over the veal.

Mushroom-Veal Stew

If you make this ahead of time, and you certainly can, add the sour cream just before eating.

½ pound veal stew meat, cubed
2 tablespoons butter
1 small onion, quartered
¼ teaspoon salt
Freshly ground pepper
⅓ cup beef bouillon
6–8 mushrooms, sliced
1½ teaspoons flour
3 tablespoons sour cream
Chopped parsley

Brown the veal quickly in 1 tablespoon of the butter. Add the onion pieces and cook them over low heat for about 10 minutes. Add the salt, pepper and bouillon, bring to a boil, cover and simmer for 1 hour, or until the meat is tender.

Sauté the mushrooms lightly in the remaining table-spoon of butter and add them to the veal. Mix the flour with a little cold water and stir it into the mixture. Cook, stirring, until thickened. Add the sour cream and bring almost to a boil. Sprinkle with parsley.

Barbecued Lamb Chop

1 thick shoulder lamb chop
Barbecue Sauce (p. 196)

Brush the lamb chop with the barbecue sauce. Broil about 3 or 4 inches from the heat, allowing 5–7 minutes for each side and brushing frequently with the sauce.

Skillet Lamb Chop

Meat and vegetables in one pot.

1 thick lamb chop
½ clove garlic
1 tablespoon butter or oil
Salt
Freshly ground pepper
1 potato, peeled and quartered
1 small green pepper, seeded and quartered
4 small white onions, canned or cooked

Rub the chop well with the garlic. Brown it lightly on both sides in the hot butter. Season with salt and pepper, add the potato, green pepper and onions, cover and cook over low heat for 30 minutes, or until the vegetables are tender. Taste and adjust the seasonings before eating.

Lamb Chop with Artichoke

A Roman specialty.

1 medium artichoke
2 cups water
1 tablespoon lemon juice or vinegar
2 tablespoons olive oil
1 large lamb chop, trimmed
Salt
Freshly ground pepper
1 small clove garlic, minced
¼ teaspoon rosemary
1 can (8 ounces) plum tomatoes

Tear the tough outer leaves from the artichoke and trim the stem to ½ inch. Using a sharp knife, cut off the very top of the artichoke. Cut the artichoke into quarters and remove the chokes. Drop the artichoke pieces into the water and lemon juice to prevent them from darkening. Bring some salted water to a boil and parboil the artichoke pieces for about 8–10 minutes.

Heat the olive oil in a skillet and brown the lamb chop on both sides. Pour off the excess fat. Arrange the artichoke pieces around the meat. Add the salt, pepper, garlic, rosemary and tomatoes. Bring to a boil, cover and simmer for about 30 minutes, or until the meat and artichoke pieces are tender. If the sauce seems too thin, cook it rapidly, uncovered, for about 5–10 minutes until it is reduced.

Lamb Chop with Apples and Potatoes

Warmly satisfying when you're alone on a cold winter night.

1 thick lamb chop, trimmed
1 tablespoon butter
2 medium potatoes, peeled and sliced thin
1 medium onion, sliced thin
Salt
Freshly ground pepper
1 apple, peeled, cored and quartered
1 teaspoon flour
½ cup bouillon
3 tablespoons apple juice or cider

Preheat the oven to 375°.

Brown the chop quickly on both sides in the hot butter; remove from skillet and keep warm. Cook the potatoes and onion in the same butter until golden. Put them in a small buttered baking dish and top with the lamb chop. Season with salt and pepper to taste, and arrange the apple pieces on top.

Sprinkle the flour in the frying pan in which the chop and vegetables were browned and cook until medium brown. Pour in the bouillon and bring to a boil, stirring constantly. Stir in the apple juice, then pour the mixture over the baking-dish ingredients. Bake for about 45 minutes, or until the meat is done and the potatoes are tender.

Lamb Shank Milanaise

Cook this the night before if it's more convenient.

1 lamb shank, trimmed
Salt
Freshly ground pepper
1 tablespoon flour
1 tablespoon butter
½ cup dry white wine
¼ cup hot bouillon
1 teaspoon chopped parsley
½ small clove garlic, minced
1 teaspoon grated lemon rind

Season the lamb shank with salt and pepper and dust it with flour. Heat the butter in a small skillet and brown the lamb in it on all sides; pour off any excess butter. Pour the wine over the lamb and cook, uncovered, over medium heat for 5 minutes. Add the bouillon, cover and cook for about 2 hours, or until tender. Ten minutes before eating, combine the parsley, garlic and lemon rind and spread it on the lamb shank. Cover and cook 10 minutes more.

Turkish Lamb Pilaf

If you have extra meat, save it or freeze it to use in other lamb dishes, such as Lamb in White Wine (p. 82) or Bigos (p. 83).

1 tablespoon butter
¼ pound boneless lamb, in julienne strips
½ onion, chopped fine
2 teaspoons pine nuts or chopped walnuts
⅓ cup rice, uncooked
½ tomato, peeled, seeded and chopped
2 teaspoons currants or chopped raisins
¼ teaspoon salt
Freshly ground pepper
Pinch of ground sage
Pinch of allspice
⅔ cup boiling bouillon
Chopped parsley or mint

Heat the butter and sauté the lamb strips in it until golden brown; remove and keep warm. Cook the onion in the same butter until soft. Add the nuts and rice and cook over medium heat for 5 minutes, stirring constantly. Add the tomato, currants, salt, pepper, sage, allspice and bouillon. Blend thoroughly, then cover tightly. Cook over the lowest heat possible until the rice is tender and the liquid is absorbed, about 20–25 minutes; do not stir. Return the lamb strips to the pot and heat through. Let stand, covered, in a warm place without cooking for about 15 minutes. Sprinkle with parsley or mint before eating.

Lamb in White Wine

Add the beaten egg at the last minute, just before you sit down to eat.

½ pound boneless lamb shoulder, cut in pieces and
   trimmed
Salt
Freshly ground pepper
½ garlic clove, minced
2 teaspoons olive oil
3 tablespoons dry white wine
¼ teaspoon dried rosemary
Dash of Tabasco sauce
½ teaspoon grated lemon rind
1 egg, beaten

Season the lamb with salt and pepper. Sauté the garlic in the oil for a minute or two, then add the lamb and brown over medium heat. Add the wine, rosemary and Tabasco sauce. Bring to a boil, cover and simmer over low heat for about 45 minutes to 1 hour, until the lamb is tender, stirring occasionally and adding a little more wine if necessary. Just before eating, add the lamb broth and lemon rind to the beaten egg, then pour over the lamb and heat to thicken; do not boil.

Bigos

This Polish dish is especially useful when you have a little leftover cooked lamb.

1 strip bacon, diced
½ small onion, minced
1 cup sauerkraut
Salt
Freshly ground pepper
1 teaspoon caraway seed
½ cup diced cooked lamb
1 small Italian sausage (hot or mild) or 1 small piece of
    Polish sausage

Cook the bacon until it is limp. In the same skillet, sauté the onion until golden. Add the sauerkraut, salt, pepper and caraway seed and heat thoroughly. Add the lamb, cover and cook over low heat for 15 minutes. Meanwhile, slice the sausage and fry it in its own fat. Add it to the lamb mixture and stir to combine well.

Lamb-and-Carrot Patty

This is also delicious when made with ground beef.

¼ pound ground lamb
¼ cup grated raw carrot
1 teaspoon minced green onion
1 tablespoon cold water
¼ teaspoon salt
Freshly ground pepper
⅛ teaspoon crushed rosemary leaves
1 tablespoon chili sauce
1½ teaspoons lemon juice
¼ teaspoon dry mustard
1 teaspoon chopped parsley
Dash of Worcestershire sauce

Combine the lamb, carrot, onion, water, salt, pepper and rosemary. Mix well and shape into 1 or 2 patties. Broil about 4 or 5 inches from the heat, allowing 5 minutes for each side.

Meanwhile, combine the rest of the ingredients in a small saucepan. Heat, stirring, for about 5 minutes, then pour over the hot patty or patties and eat at once.

Lamb Kidney Stew

2 lamb kidneys
Milk
1½ tablespoons butter
6 mushrooms, sliced
2 teaspoons chopped parsley
1 teaspoon grated onion
1 tablespoon sherry
2 tablespoons heavy cream
Salt
Freshly ground pepper
Buttered toast

Split the kidneys in two and remove the white membrane and cord. Soak for 10 minutes in milk to cover, then drain and dry. Cut in thin slices and sauté in butter, together with the sliced mushrooms. Add the parsley and onion and simmer over low heat for 5 minutes. Add the sherry and cream and simmer 2 minutes longer. Season to taste with salt and pepper and eat at once on buttered toast.

Braised Pork Chop

A Chinese-style dish for one.

1 large pork chop (or 2 small)
3 tablespoons soy sauce
1½ teaspoons sherry
½ small clove garlic, minced
1 slice fresh gingerroot, minced
1–2 teaspoons vegetable oil
1 green onion, cut in 1-inch pieces
1 teaspoon sugar
Freshly ground pepper

Remove the bone from the pork chop. Mix 1 tablespoon of the soy sauce with the sherry, garlic and gingerroot. Let the pork marinate in this mixture for 30 minutes, then drain. Fry the chop slowly in oil until golden brown. Mix the remaining 2 tablespoons of the soy sauce with the green onion, sugar and pepper to taste. Pour over the chop, cover and simmer for 30 minutes.

Hungarian Pork Chop

This has a savory sour-cream-and-paprika sauce.

1 large pork chop, trimmed
Salt
Freshly ground pepper
½ onion, chopped
½ clove garlic, minced
1–2 tablespoons butter
½ bay leaf
¼ cup chicken broth
⅓ cup sour cream
½ teaspoon paprika

Sprinkle the pork chop with salt and pepper. Sauté the onion and garlic in hot butter until soft. Push to one side of the skillet, add the pork chop and brown quickly on both sides. Pour off the fat. Stir in the bay leaf and chicken broth, cover and cook over low heat for about 1 hour. Remove the chop to a serving plate and keep warm.

Cook the pan juices over high heat for 5–10 minutes to reduce them. Turn off the heat and stir in the sour cream and paprika. Heat through, but do not boil, then pour over the chop.

Lemon-Celery Pork Chop

1 large, thick pork chop
½ clove garlic
¼ teaspoon grated lemon rind
Flour
About 2 tablespoons butter
1 cup sliced celery
Salt
Freshly ground pepper
1 teaspoon lemon juice

Rub the pork chop with the cut side of the garlic and the lemon rind. Coat it lightly with flour. Sauté in a tablespoon or more of butter until cooked through and lightly browned. Add the celery, dot with more butter, cover and cook over low heat for about 10 minutes, or until the celery is crisp-tender. Season with salt, pepper and lemon juice and eat at once.

Orange-Baked Pork Chop

1 thick pork chop
Salt
Freshly ground pepper
1 teaspoon flour
½ orange, sliced thin
2 tablespoons orange juice

Preheat oven to 350°.

Put the chop in a small casserole. Season it generously with salt and pepper, sprinkle it with flour and top with the orange slices. Pour the orange juice over all, cover and bake for 1 hour or more, until tender and cooked through.

Pork-Vegetable Skillet

A complete meal for one in a single skillet.

1 pork chop
About ¼ cup beef bouillon
1 medium potato, peeled and halved lengthwise
1 carrot, scraped
½ green pepper, in chunks
Salt
Freshly ground pepper

Brown the pork chop in its own fat over medium heat. Push it to one side of the skillet and add the bouillon, potato and carrot. Put the green pepper chunks on the pork chop, season everything with salt and pepper, cover and simmer for about 45 minutes, until the vegetables and chop are tender, adding more bouillon if necessary.

Italian Stewed Pork with Celery

½ clove garlic, peeled
1 tablespoon olive oil
½ small carrot, chopped
½ pound lean pork, in bite-sized pieces
¼ cup dry red or white wine
½ teaspoon salt
Freshly ground pepper
½ cup thinly sliced celery
1 tomato, peeled and chopped

Brown the garlic in the oil; discard the garlic. Add the
carrot, pork, wine, salt and pepper, cover and cook over
low heat for 45 minutes. Add the celery and tomato and
cook for another ½ hour, or until the meat and vegetables
are tender. Taste and adjust seasonings before eating.

Pork-Zucchini Stir-Fry

A quick, easy dish for the end of a busy day. If possible, have the butcher cut the pork for you.

¼ pound boneless pork, in julienne strips
2 tablespoons chopped onion
1 tablespoon oil
½ cup sliced zucchini
6 mushrooms, sliced
¼ teaspoon marjoram
¼ teaspoon salt
Freshly ground pepper
2 tablespoons beef broth
Cooked rice

Sauté the pork and onion in the oil over high heat until the pork is lightly browned. Add the zucchini, mushrooms, marjoram, salt, pepper and broth. Cook, stirring, for 5–10 minutes or until the vegetables are tender and the pork is cooked through. Eat with cooked rice.

Sweet-and-Pungent Pork

¼–½ pound lean pork, in ½-inch cubes
1 tablespoon vegetable oil
1 small green pepper, seeded and sliced
⅔ cup sliced apples
¼ cup chicken broth
2 teaspoons cornstarch
1–2 teaspoons soy sauce
2 tablespoons vinegar
2 tablespoons sugar
Salt
Freshly ground pepper
Hot rice

Brown the pork on all sides in the hot oil. Add the green pepper, apples and 2 tablespoons of the broth. Bring to a boil, cover and simmer for about 30–40 minutes, stirring frequently, until done.

Meanwhile, blend the remaining 2 tablespoons of the broth with the cornstarch, soy sauce, vinegar, sugar, salt and pepper, and mix until smooth. Add slowly to the pork mixture and cook, stirring, until the mixture thickens. Spoon over hot rice.

Curried Pork

1 tablespoon flour
Salt
Freshly ground pepper
Generous pinch of ground ginger
¼–½ pound lean pork, in 1-inch cubes
1 tablespoon butter
½ teaspoon curry powder
Pinch of chili powder
3 tablespoons chopped onion
2 tablespoons chopped green pepper
⅓ cup hot bouillon

Combine the flour, salt, pepper and ginger. Dredge the pork in this mixture, then brown it on all sides in the hot butter, stirring occasionally. Stir in the rest of the ingredients. Bring to a boil, cover and simmer, stirring occasionally, for 1¼ to 1½ hours, or until the pork is tender. Adjust the seasonings with salt and or curry powder if necessary.

Ma Ho

A pork dish from Thailand.

Lettuce leaves
5 ounces canned mandarin oranges, drained
½ clove garlic, minced
1½ teaspoons oil
⅓ cup diced pork
1–2 tablespoons finely chopped peanuts
1½ teaspoons sugar
1½ teaspoons soy sauce
1½ teaspoons water
Salt
Cayenne pepper

Arrange several lettuce leaves on a plate, top with the orange slices and chill.

Sauté the garlic in the hot oil until golden. Add the pork and stir-fry until brown and almost done. Add the rest of the ingredients, and continue to stir-fry until the pork is done and the ingredients well mixed. Pour over the oranges and eat at once.

Sweet-and-Sour Spareribs

¾ pound spareribs
2 teaspoons flour
¼ cup diced celery
¼ cup chopped green pepper
½ small onion, chopped
2 tablespoons maple-flavored syrup
4 ounces canned pineapple chunks with syrup
1 tablespoon vinegar
1½ tablespoons soy sauce
Salt
Freshly ground pepper
Cornstarch (optional)

Preheat the oven to 400°.

Roast the spareribs for 30 minutes, or until golden brown, turning occasionally. Remove the ribs from the roasting pan and pour off all but 1 tablespoon of the drippings. Over low heat on the stove, blend the flour into the drippings, then stir in the celery, green pepper, onion, syrup, pineapple, vinegar, soy sauce, salt and pepper. Mix well, then add the ribs and bake at 375° for 1½ hours, or until the ribs are tender, basting every 20 minutes. Put the ribs on a plate and pour the sauce over them. If necessary, thicken the sauce first by adding 1 tablespoon of cornstarch mixed with a little cold water and heating the sauce until it thickens.

Savory Country-Style Ribs

¾ pound country-style pork ribs
Prepared mustard
3 tablespoons soft bread crumbs

Preheat the oven to 350°.
Spread each rib with mustard and roll it in some crumbs.
Roast for 1½ to 2 hours, or until well browned and crisp.

Glazed Ham Steak

What could be simpler—or more delicious?

½-pound ready-to-eat ham slice
Butter
2 teaspoons orange marmalade
½ teaspoon dry mustard

Brown the ham slice on both sides in butter in a heavy skillet. Mix the marmalade and mustard and spread half on each side of the ham. Cook about 2 minutes more.

Baked Ham Slice with Apple Rings

½-pound ready-to-eat ham slice
¼ cup packed brown sugar
¼ teaspoon ground cloves
¼ teaspoon cinnamon
1 tart apple, peeled and cored, in ½-inch slices
3 tablespoons pineapple juice

Preheat the oven to 350°.

Gash the fat in the ham slice to prevent it from curling. Mix the brown sugar, cloves and cinnamon, and rub ¼ of the mixture into one side of the ham. Place the ham, sugar side down, in a small shallow baking dish. Arrange the apple slices around the ham. Sprinkle the apples and ham with the remaining sugar mixture. Heat the juice to boiling and pour it over all. Bake, uncovered, for about 30–45 minutes, depending on the thickness of the ham. Remove the ham and apples to a plate and pour the juices over all.

Southern-Style Ham Steak

Eat this with a corn muffin or some grits.

½-pound ready-to-eat ham slice
1 tablespoon brown sugar
1 tablespoon flour
Butter (optional)
½ cup milk
2 tablespoons chopped parsley

Trim the excess fat from the ham and melt the fat in a skillet. Mix in the brown sugar and flour and sprinkle half the mixture over the ham slice, pressing it in. Turn the ham and repeat on the other side. Brown the ham in the hot fat on both sides until golden, adding a little butter if necessary. Add the milk to the skillet, scraping any brown bits from the bottom. Cover and simmer for 20–30 minutes, or until the ham is tender. Stir in the parsley.

Ham-Zucchini Skillet

An easy, one-pot, last-minute meal.

1 small onion, sliced
1 tablespoon vegetable oil
½ cup cooked ham, in small pieces
1 small zucchini, diced
Salt
Freshly ground pepper

Cook the onion in the hot oil for about 3 minutes. Add the ham, zucchini, salt and pepper, and stir-fry over medium-high heat for about 10 minutes until the ham is lightly browned and the zucchini crisp-tender.

Home-fried Ham and Potato

The secret here is slow cooking and lots of butter.

1 small onion, sliced
About 2 tablespoons butter
½ cup sliced cooked potato
½ cup ham pieces
Salt
Freshly ground pepper
Paprika

Cook the onion in 1 tablespoon of the butter until lightly browned. Add the potato and ham and cook slowly, over medium-low heat, until lightly browned, adding more butter as necessary. Season to taste with salt, pepper and paprika, and turn several times with a wide spatula.

Skillet Ham and Sweet Potato

Skillet meals make sense when you are cooking just for yourself.

1 tablespoon minced onion
1½ tablespoons butter
2 teaspoons flour
2 ounces canned pineapple chunks and syrup
2 tablespoons packed brown sugar
½ cup diced ham
1 cup sliced cooked sweet potato

Cook the onion in the butter for 2 or 3 minutes. Blend in the flour and cook for another few minutes, stirring. Gradually add 3 tablespoons pineapple syrup or water (or a mixture of both) and cook, stirring, until thickened. Add the pineapple, sugar and ham. Arrange the sweet potato slices on top. Bring to a boil, cover and simmer for 10 minutes, or until heated through.

Curried Ham

Eat this on hot cooked rice mixed with freshly grated orange rind.

2 tablespoons chopped onion
2 teaspoons butter
2 teaspoons flour
⅓ cup chicken broth
4 ounces canned pineapple chunks with syrup
1½ teaspoons chopped chutney
1 teaspoon curry powder
Salt
Freshly ground pepper
½ cup ham pieces

Sauté the onion in the hot butter for 2 or 3 minutes. Add the flour and cook for another 2 or 3 minutes, stirring. Gradually mix in the broth and some of the pineapple syrup, stirring until thickened. Blend in the chutney, curry powder, salt and pepper and simmer for 10 minutes, thinning if necessary with a little more broth. Taste and adjust the seasonings. Add the pineapple and the ham, and heat thoroughly.

Breaded Pigs' Knuckles

2 pigs' knuckles
1 small onion, stuck with 2 cloves
1 teaspoon salt
1 egg, beaten
Bread crumbs
Vegetable oil or shortening

Put the pigs' knuckles in a pot filled with enough boiling water to cover them; boil for 15 minutes. Remove them with a slotted spoon; reserve the liquid. Plunge the knuckles into cold water, then pull off the skin. Return the knuckles to the pot, and add the onion and salt. Cook, covered, until the meat falls off the bones, about 2 hours. Drain.

Pick the meat off the bones and cut into bite-sized pieces. Dip in the egg and then in the bread crumbs. Heat the oil or shortening and sauté the meat on all sides until golden brown.

Sausage and Apple Rings

2 brown-and-serve sausages
1 apple, cored and cut in rings
1 tablespoon packed brown sugar
1 tablespoon water

Brown the sausages lightly in an ungreased skillet. Add the apple rings, brown sugar and water. Cover and cook for 10 minutes, until the apples are fork-tender.

Pepperoni and Peppers

Try this easy, peppy dish when your appetite needs a little lift. It's good alone or served over pasta or rice.

½ cup thin green-pepper strips
¼ cup chopped onion
1–2 tablespoons butter or oil
¼ pound pepperoni, sliced thin
½ cup canned tomatoes, cut up
Salt
Freshly ground pepper
Freshly grated Parmesan cheese

Sauté the green pepper and onion in hot butter until crisp-tender. Stir in the pepperoni and cook for 2 minutes. Add the tomatoes and salt. Simmer for 5 minutes, or a little longer if you wish. Sprinkle with Parmesan cheese before eating.

CHICKEN and CHICKEN LIVERS

○)

CHICKEN IS PERFECT "SINGLES" FOOD: easy to prepare and inexpensive, it goes well with many other kinds of foods and lends itself to a variety of dishes, both plain and elegant. Most important to the solitary eater, chicken is readily available in small quantities and you are free to select the parts of the chicken that you really prefer.

White-meat eaters will want the breasts or wings. Both will cook faster than dark meat, if speed is a consideration. Boned chicken breasts, or "chicken cutlets," as they are sometimes called in supermarkets, cook fastest of all, yet are the basis for some of the more delicate and luxurious dishes around.

If you prefer dark meat, buy chicken thighs and legs. Dark meat takes a bit longer to cook and has a deeper chicken flavor than white meat.

Chicken backs and necks, often packaged separately, are good for making stock, which can be used as a basis for soups or as a soup itself (see Chicken Soup, p. 9).

Stock is also important to many sauces. Try poaching some chicken in homemade chicken stock, letting the chicken simmer gently just until it is tender. This will give you two rewards: an extra rich stock for soups and sauces, and some well-flavored, juicy cooked chicken to use hot in pilafs, curries and other cooked-chicken recipes, or cold in sandwiches and salads. You can also poach chicken in canned chicken broth with very satisfactory results.

Another way to make sure you have some cooked chicken around is to cook a little extra in whatever recipe you are making. Cut the leftover chicken into strips or cubes and freeze it for use in a cooked-chicken dish.

Chicken livers are also available in small quantities, and any extras can be frozen for use in another meal. Rich and nutritious, chicken livers also require very little cooking time.

Baked Chicken Quarter

1 chicken quarter (¾–1 pound)
¼ teaspoon salt
Freshly ground pepper
2 teaspoons butter
2 tablespoons chopped celery
1 tablespoon water
⅛ teaspoon dried tarragon
1 tablespoon toasted slivered almonds

Preheat the oven to 375°.

Sprinkle the chicken with salt and pepper. Place, skin side up, in a small shallow baking pan. Melt the butter in a small saucepan, add the celery, water and tarragon, and spoon over the chicken. Bake, uncovered, basting occasionally, until tender, about 1 hour. Sprinkle with the almonds during the last 5 minutes of baking.

Baked Orange Chicken

If you double the amount of chicken in this dish, you will have enough left over for Curried Chicken (p. 117).

1 chicken quarter (¾–1 pound)
1½ tablespoons butter
½ orange, sliced crosswise
2 teaspoons flour
Salt
Dash of cinnamon
½ cup orange juice

Preheat the oven to 375°.

Brown the chicken in the butter in a skillet. Arrange the chicken and orange slices in a small shallow baking dish. Blend the flour, salt and cinnamon into the skillet juices, stirring well for a few minutes over low heat. Gradually stir in the orange juice and cook over medium heat, stirring, until the juice boils and thickens. Pour over the chicken and bake for about 45 minutes, or until the chicken is tender.

Chicken Victoria

¾–1 pound chicken parts
2 teaspoons flour
¼ teaspoon salt
Freshly ground pepper
2 tablespoons slivered blanched almonds
1½ tablespoons oil
¼ cup chopped onion
⅓ cup chopped celery
½ small clove garlic, minced
4–6 sliced mushrooms
1½ tablespoons chopped parsley
¼ cup dry sherry

Dredge the chicken in a mixture of the flour, salt and pepper. Brown the almonds lightly in the oil in a small skillet. Remove the almonds, then brown the chicken on all sides in the remaining oil; remove the chicken. Add to the skillet the onion, celery, garlic, mushrooms and 1 tablespoon of the parsley. Cook for 2 or 3 minutes, then pour in the sherry and bring to a boil. Add the chicken, cover and simmer for about 45 minutes, or until tender. Sprinkle with the almonds and the remaining parsley before eating.

Broiled Lemon Chicken

¾–1 pound chicken parts
1 tablespoon oil
1 small clove garlic, minced
Grated peel and juice of 1 lemon
¼ teaspoon thyme
Pinch of sage
Salt
Freshly ground pepper

Place the chicken on a broiler pan. Mix the oil with the garlic and brush on the chicken. Sprinkle with the lemon peel and juice, thyme, sage, salt and pepper. Broil about 6 inches from the heat, turning occasionally and basting frequently with the pan juices, until the chicken is brown and tender, about 30–40 minutes. Lower the broiler pan if the chicken browns too quickly.

Broiled Mustard-and-Honey-Glazed Chicken

¾–1 pound chicken parts
1 large clove garlic, minced
Salt
2 teaspoons prepared mustard
2 tablespoons honey
1 tablespoon lime or lemon juice

Rub the chicken well all over with the garlic. Sprinkle with salt. Place, skin side down, on a broiler pan and spread with half the mustard. Mix the honey and the lime juice. Broil the chicken about 6 inches from the heat for about 20 minutes, basting twice with the honey mixture during the last 10 minutes. Turn the chicken skin side up, spread with the remaining mustard and broil for another 20 minutes, or until the chicken is tender, basting with the remaining honey mixture during the last 10 minutes.

Sesame Fried Chicken

2 tablespoons flour
1 tablespoon sesame seed
¼ teaspoon salt
¼ teaspoon paprika
¼ teaspoon poultry seasoning
Freshly ground pepper
¾–1 pound chicken parts, cut up
Oil or fat for frying

Mix the flour, sesame seed, salt, paprika, poultry seasoning and pepper. Roll damp chicken pieces in the mixture.
Heat ½ inch of oil or fat in a skillet. Fry the chicken in
the fat, uncovered, allowing 15–25 minutes for each side,
until tender and brown.

Chicken and Rice Skillet

There's a Chinese feeling to this one-pot meal.

2 teaspoons oil
4 teaspoons soy sauce
½ onion, chopped
½ clove garlic, minced
¾–1 pound chicken parts, cut small
½ teaspoon ginger
Freshly ground pepper
1¼ cups hot water
1 chicken bouillon cube
½ cup rice

Heat the oil, soy sauce, onion and garlic in a skillet. Add
the chicken and brown slowly over medium-low heat for
about 15 minutes. Season with ginger and pepper. Push
the chicken to the center of the skillet. Pour the water
into the pan, then add the bouillon cube and the rice.
Cover and simmer until the rice is done, about 20 minutes.

Barbecued Chicken Legs

2 chicken legs
2 tablespoons lemon juice
2 teaspoons oil
Pinch of rosemary
Pinch of thyme
Pinch of marjoram
Salt
Freshly ground pepper
Celery seed

Put the chicken on a greased broiler pan. Mix the remaining ingredients together and brush the chicken with them. Broil about 3–4 inches from the heat for about 30 minutes, brushing frequently with the sauce. Turn and, basting again, broil for about 15 minutes more, or until tender.

Chicken Breast Gruyère

Simple to prepare, yet rich and elegant, this is a good dish to make when you want to pamper yourself a bit.

1 small whole chicken breast, skinned, split and boned
Salt
Freshly ground pepper
2 tablespoons butter
4 mushrooms, chopped
1 tablespoon flour
⅔ cup milk
½ cup (about 2 ounces) shredded Gruyère or Swiss cheese

Sprinkle the chicken breasts with salt and pepper. Melt 1 tablespoon of the butter in a small skillet and sauté the chicken in it, turning several times, until done, about 10 minutes. Remove to a broilerproof platter. Sauté the mushrooms in the same skillet for about 5 minutes, then spoon them over the chicken.

Melt the remaining tablespoon of butter in the skillet, scraping any brown bits from the bottom. Blend in the flour and cook over low heat, stirring, for about 2 minutes. Slowly pour in the milk and simmer until thickened, stirring constantly. Blend in the cheese and cook until melted, then add salt and pepper to taste; the sauce should be very thick. Spoon over the chicken and put under the broiler until brown and bubbly.

Chicken Breast Beau Séjour

1 small whole chicken breast, skinned, split and boned
Flour
1 tablespoon butter
1 tablespoon oil
2 cloves garlic
1 bay leaf, broken in half
Pinch of thyme
Salt
Freshly ground pepper
1½ tablespoons wine vinegar
1 chicken bouillon cube, dissolved in ¼ cup boiling water

Coat the chicken with flour. Cook it in hot butter and oil until golden. Lower the heat, place garlic and bay leaf on each breast half and season with thyme, salt and pepper. Sauté slowly, turning once, until tender, about 10 minutes.

Transfer the chicken to a warm plate, leaving the garlic and bay leaf in the skillet. Add the vinegar and cook over high heat until it evaporates. Add the bouillon and simmer 5 minutes more. Remove the garlic and bay leaf and pour the sauce over the chicken.

Walnut Chicken

A Chinese feast for one.

1 small whole chicken breast, skinned, split and boned
1 tablespoon cornstarch
1 egg white, unbeaten
½ cup walnut meats
Oil for deep-frying
2–3 tablespoons vegetable oil
½ cup diced celery
2 ounces water chestnuts
3 tablespoons chicken broth
1½ tablespoons soy sauce
1½ teaspoons sherry
½ teaspoon sugar
1–2 slices fresh gingerroot, minced
Hot cooked rice (optional)

Cube the chicken meat. Mix 1½ teaspoons of the cornstarch with 1½ teaspoons water and beat into the egg white with a fork. Add the chicken and mix until each piece is coated. Put the walnuts in water to cover and boil for 3 minutes. Drain and dry, then deep-fry in hot oil (375° on a frying thermometer) until golden brown.

Heat the vegetable oil in another pan. Add the chicken, celery and water chestnuts and fry for 3 or 4 minutes. Mix together the broth, soy sauce, sherry, sugar, gingerroot and the remaining 1½ teaspoons of cornstarch. Add to the chicken mixture and cook, stirring, until thickened. Sprinkle the walnuts over the top and eat with rice if you wish.

Chicken-Ham Rolls

A package of sliced ham will go a long way if you use it in clever dishes like this.

½ chicken breast, skinned and boned
2½ tablespoons butter
4 thin slices boiled ham
1 tablespoon flour
½ cup milk
¼ cup (about 1 ounce) shredded sharp Cheddar cheese
3 tablespoons dry white wine
Chopped parsley

Preheat the oven to 350°.

Sauté the chicken in 1½ tablespoons of the butter until golden, allowing about 6 minutes on each side. Cool, then cut in 4 fingerlike strips. Put one strip on each ham slice, roll up and arrange in a small shallow baking dish.

Melt the remaining tablespoon of butter in the same skillet, mix in the flour and cook over low heat, stirring, for 2 or 3 minutes. Add the milk and cook, stirring, until thickened. Blend in the cheese, then remove from the heat and add the wine. Pour over the rolls and bake for about 30 minutes. Sprinkle with parsley before eating.

Chicken Pilaf

Make this when you have some leftover cooked chicken on hand.

½ cup cooked chicken, in strips
2 tablespoons butter
2 teaspoons minced onion
2 tablespoons coarsely chopped walnuts
Salt
Freshly ground pepper
Pinch of ground coriander or thyme
½ cup uncooked rice
1 cup chicken broth
1 small tomato, peeled, seeded and chopped

Sauté the chicken in the butter in a skillet for a minute or two, then add the onion and walnuts, and cook about

3 minutes more. Season to taste with salt, pepper and coriander. Add the rice and cook over medium heat, stirring, for 5 minutes. Pour in the chicken broth and tomato, bring to a boil, cover and simmer, without stirring, until the rice is cooked and the liquid all absorbed, about 20 minutes. Turn off the heat and let stand for 5 minutes before eating.

Curried Chicken

This is a quick, easy and cheerfully spicy dish.

1 tablespoon butter
1 teaspoon curry powder
1 tablespoon flour
¾ cup chicken broth
3 tablespoons golden raisins
½ cup diced cooked chicken
Salt
Freshly ground pepper
Hot cooked rice
Toasted slivered almonds

Melt the butter in a saucepan over low heat. Add the curry powder and flour, and cook, stirring, for about 3 minutes. Gradually pour in the broth and cook, stirring, until smooth and thickened. Add the raisins and simmer, stirring occasionally, for 8–10 minutes. Mix in the chicken and heat gently, seasoning to taste with salt and pepper, and with more curry powder if you wish. Spoon over hot rice and sprinkle with almonds.

Chicken with Green Peppers

If you have any water chestnuts left over after making this dish, drain them. Mix cold water with enough salt to make a salty solution, put the mixture in a jar and add the water chestnuts. Stored like this in the refrigerator, they will keep for many months.

½ cup diced, cooked chicken
1 teaspoon cornstarch
1 teaspoon dry sherry
Salt
1 tablespoon cold water
1½ tablespoons oil
½ clove garlic, minced
1–2 ounces diced water chestnuts
1 small green pepper, diced

Mix the chicken with ½ teaspoon of the cornstarch, the sherry and salt; set aside. Blend the remaining cornstarch and the cold water; set aside.

Heat the oil in a skillet, add the garlic and the chicken mixture and cook over medium-high heat, stirring, for 2 minutes. Mix in the water chestnuts and the green pepper. Add the cornstarch mixture and cook, stirring until just thickened.

Broiled Cornish Hen

1 Rock Cornish hen, split
Salt
Freshly ground pepper
½ teaspoon dried marjoram or thyme
1 tablespoon melted butter

Rub the hen all over with salt, pepper and marjoram, and let it stand for about 1 hour. Place, skin side down, on a broiler pan. Brush with some of the melted butter and broil about 5 inches from the heat for 12–15 minutes. Turn, brush again with melted butter and broil 12–15 minutes more, or until tender and well browned.

Chicken Livers Stroganoff

1 slice bacon
¼ cup sliced onions
1 tablespoon flour
¼ teaspoon paprika
⅛ teaspoon salt
¼ pound chicken livers
2 tablespoons chicken broth
6 sliced mushrooms
2 tablespoons sour cream
1 tablespoon water
Hot cooked noodles

Cook the bacon until crisp; drain, crumble and set aside. Sauté the onions in the bacon drippings until limp, but not browned; remove from the pan and set aside.

Mix 2 teaspoons of the flour with the paprika and salt, and dredge the livers in the mixture. Brown them lightly in the bacon drippings. Drain off any remaining fat in the skillet. Pour in the chicken broth and scrape the bottom of the pan. Add the mushrooms and onions, cover and simmer for about 10 minutes. Remove the livers, mushrooms and onions from the pan.

Blend the remaining teaspoon of the flour with the sour cream and 1 tablespoon of water. Mix into the pan drippings and cook, stirring, until thickened. Return the livers, mushrooms, onions and the reserved bacon to the sauce, heat gently, then spoon over hot noodles and eat at once.

Chicken Livers and Barley

½ onion, minced
2 tablespoons butter
6 sliced mushrooms
¼ cup quick-cooking medium barley
½ cup chicken broth
¼ pound chicken livers
Salt
Freshly ground pepper

Brown the onion lightly in 1 tablespoon of the butter. Add the mushrooms and sauté for 5 minutes. Add the barley and brown lightly, stirring. Pour in the broth, bring to a boil and season with salt and pepper. Cover and simmer for about 25 minutes, or until the barley is tender and the liquid absorbed.

Meanwhile, sauté the chicken livers in the remaining butter and season with salt and pepper, then mix them into the cooked barley and eat at once.

Braised Chicken Livers with Brown Rice

¼ pound chicken livers
2 tablespoons flour
2 teaspoons butter
¼ cup chicken broth
Salt
Freshly ground pepper
Rosemary
Hot cooked brown rice
Chopped parsley

Dredge the chicken livers in the flour. Brown them lightly in the butter in a skillet. Add the broth and some salt, pepper and rosemary. Scrape the bottom of the pan well, then cover and simmer for about 10 minutes. Spoon over the rice and sprinkle with parsley.

FISH and SHELLFISH

❀❀❀❀❀❀❀❀❀❀❀❀❀❀❀❀❀❀❀❀❀❀❀❀❀❀❀❀❀❀

◊+◊

SWEET BAY SCALLOPS, thick salmon steaks, large, juicy lobsters, jumbo shrimp—these have become delicacies in recent years, harder and harder to get and thus increasingly expensive. Some fish and most shellfish are now too dear for ordinary family fare, but if you're dining alone, you may be able to justify such an occasional treat.

Quick, simple cooking is the way with fish. It's hard to go wrong if you make sure that the fish is very, very fresh and take care not to overcook it. Fish should be juicy and tender; it is done as soon as it flakes easily with a fork and is no longer transparent.

If you use frozen fish, cook it as soon as it defrosts and never refreeze it.

Trout with Anchovy Sauce

1 tablespoon flour
Salt
Freshly ground pepper
1 trout, whole and cleaned
Olive oil
1 tablespoon butter
1–2 anchovy fillets, cut fine
2 tablespoons dry white wine
1 teaspoon chopped parsley
1 tablespoon lemon juice

Season the flour with salt and pepper. Roll the fish in the seasoned flour, then pan-fry in a small amount of hot oil until done, allowing about 5 minutes per side.

Meanwhile, melt the butter in a small saucepan, add the anchovy fillets and heat for 5 minutes. Stir in the wine and parsley, and cook 3 minutes more. Add the lemon juice. Put the fish on a plate and pour the sauce over it.

Broiled Fish Steak

You can use a fish fillet instead; it will take less time to cook, about 5 minutes.

Oil
½-pound fish steak (about ¾-inch thick)
1 tablespoon melted butter
1 teaspoon lemon juice
Salt
Freshly ground pepper

Line a broiler pan with aluminum foil and brush the foil with oil. Arrange the fish steak on the foil. Mix the melted butter and lemon juice and brush it on the fish. Season with salt and pepper. Broil about 3 inches from the heat for 8–10 minutes, or until the fish flakes easily with a fork.

Poached Cod Steak

1½ cups boiling water
1 slice lemon
1 teaspoon salt
1 slice onion
Few celery leaves or parsley sprigs
1 cod steak (about ½ pound)
2 tablespoons melted butter
2 tablespoons crumbled blue cheese
½ teaspoon vinegar
½ teaspoon prepared mustard
Dash of paprika

Combine the water, lemon, salt, onion and celery leaves in a saucepan or skillet and simmer for 10 minutes. Add the fish and simmer 10 minutes more, until the fish is tender and flakes easily with a fork. Lift the fish out onto a plate. Mix the melted butter, blue cheese, vinegar, mustard and paprika and pour over the fish.

Broiled Salmon Steak with Lemon-Dill Butter

Oil
½-pound salmon steak (about ¾-inch thick)
Salt
Pepper
1 tablespoon melted butter
¼ teaspoon grated lemon rind
1 tablespoon lemon juice
1 tablespoon chopped, fresh dill
2 lemon slices

Line a broiler pan with aluminum foil and brush the foil with oil. Sprinkle the salmon on both sides with salt and pepper, and arrange it on the foil. Mix the butter, lemon rind, lemon juice and dill, and brush some on the fish. Broil about 3 inches from the heat for 5–6 minutes, or until slightly browned. Brush again with the butter mixture, turn carefully, and brush the other side with the butter mixture. Broil for another 5–6 minutes, until the fish flakes easily with a fork. Brush with any remaining butter mixture and garnish with the lemon slices.

Cold Poached Salmon Steak

You can prepare this the night before and have it ready in the refrigerator when you get home from work. What a lovely indulgence for a hot summer evening!

About 2 cups of water
2 teaspoons white vinegar or lemon juice
2 teaspoons salt
2 onion slices
Fresh dill or parsley sprigs
3 peppercorns
½-pound salmon steak
Mayonnaise
Lemon wedges

Bring the water to a boil in a skillet and add the vinegar, salt, onion, dill and peppercorns. Carefully add the salmon steak, cover and simmer for about 6–8 minutes, or until the fish flakes easily with a fork.

Let the fish cool in the broth, then cover and chill. Before eating, put the fish on a plate, add a dollop of mayonnaise and some lemon wedges.

Golden Fish Fillet

¼-pound fish fillet
Salt
Freshly ground pepper
1 tablespoon butter
Maître d'Hôtel Butter (p. 197)

Season the fillets with salt and pepper. Sauté them in the hot butter for 3–5 minutes on each side, or until done. Pour butter over the fish and eat immediately.

Baked Fish Fillet with Potato and Onion

1 medium potato, peeled and sliced
1 small onion, peeled and sliced
1 tablespoon melted butter
¼-pound fish fillet
Bread crumbs
Paprika
Salt
Freshly ground pepper

Preheat the oven to 400°.

Put the potato and onion in a small ovenproof dish and drizzle 2 teaspoons of the butter over them. Bake for 35 minutes, or until golden, turning occasionally with a spatula.

Dip the fish in the remaining teaspoon of butter and coat it with bread crumbs. Arrange it on top of the potato mixture, season with paprika, salt and pepper and bake 15 minutes more, or until flaky.

Fish Mornay

¼-pound fillet of flounder or cod
Salt
2 teaspoons butter
2 teaspoons flour
Freshly ground pepper
½ cup milk
3 tablespoons freshly grated Parmesan cheese

Put the fish in a skillet in an inch of gently boiling salted water and simmer until it flakes easily with a fork; drain. Break the fish into large pieces and arrange them in a small broilerproof dish.

Melt the butter in a small saucepan, add the flour and cook over low heat, stirring, for about 2 minutes, seasoning to taste with salt and pepper. Slowly add the milk and cook, stirring, until thickened and bubbly. Blend in 2 tablespoons of the grated cheese. Pour the sauce over the fish, sprinkle with the remaining cheese and broil until lightly browned.

Fish Provençale

Easy and excellent, a nice treat for a lovely spring day.

¼-pound fillet of haddock, sole or flounder
Salt
Freshly ground pepper
2 teaspoons butter
1 thick slice tomato
2 thin slices onion
Parsley
Lemon wedges

Sprinkle the fish with salt and pepper. Place on a greased broiler rack, dot with 1 teaspoon of the butter and broil for 4 minutes. Turn. Top the fish with the tomato and onion. Dot with the remaining teaspoon of butter and broil 4–5 minutes more, until the fish flakes easily with a fork. Garnish with parsley and lemon wedges.

Haddock with Garlic Sauce

¼-pound fillet of haddock
Salt
Freshly ground pepper
2 tablespoons butter
1 small clove garlic, minced
1 teaspoon minced parsley
Lemon wedges
Hot cooked rice

Cut the fillet in 1-inch pieces and sprinkle with salt and pepper. Sauté the fish in 1 tablespoon of the butter until it flakes easily with a fork, about 3–5 minutes, turning carefully with a wide spatula. Remove to a heated dish and keep warm.

Melt the remaining tablespoon of butter in the same skillet and stir in the garlic. Cook for 1 minute, then pour over the fish. Sprinkle with parsley, garnish with lemon wedges and eat at once with hot rice.

Tuna in Caper Sauce

Easy to prepare at the last minute, when you don't have time to shop.

¼ cup diced celery
2 tablespoons butter
2 tablespoons flour
¼ teaspoon salt
Freshly ground pepper
½ cup milk
1 can (3½ ounces) tuna, drained and flaked
2 teaspoons capers
Chopped parsley
Hot cooked rice

Cook the celery in a small amount of boiling salted water for 5 minutes; drain. Melt the butter, then blend in the flour, salt and pepper and cook over low heat, stirring, for about 2 minutes. Gradually add the milk and cook over medium heat, stirring, until smooth and thickened. Add the tuna, celery and capers and heat thoroughly. Sprinkle with parsley and spoon over rice.

Tuna with Rice and Peas

2 tablespoons minced onion
2 tablespoons butter
1 can (3½ ounces) tuna, drained and flaked
½ cup hot cooked peas
½ cup hot cooked rice
Salt
Freshly ground pepper
Freshly grated Parmesan or Romano cheese

Sauté the onion in the butter until soft. Add the tuna, peas and rice to the skillet, season to taste with salt and pepper and heat thoroughly. Sprinkle with grated cheese just before eating.

Salmon Patties

A dinner to fix when you haven't planned ahead—all the ingredients should be readily at hand.

About 2 tablespoons butter
½ small onion, minced
1 can (3¾ ounces) salmon
¼ teaspoon salt
¼ teaspoon dry mustard
1 tablespoon chopped parsley
1 egg, slightly beaten
1 cup soft bread crumbs
Flour
Tartar Sauce (p. 200)

Melt 1 tablespoon of the butter in a skillet. Add the onion and sauté for 2–3 minutes. Remove from the heat. Add the salmon, including the liquid, and the salt, mustard and parsley. Mix well, then stir in the egg and the crumbs.

Shape into 2 large flat patties. Dredge in flour, then sauté in 1 tablespoon or more of butter until browned on both sides and heated through. Eat with tartar sauce.

Steamed Clams

With some dishes, there's an unexpected advantage to eating alone: you can dig in and not worry about how messy you get.

1 quart soft-shelled clams
2 tablespoons water
Melted butter

Scrub the clam shells thoroughly with a brush, changing the water repeatedly until there is no trace of sand. Put the clams in a deep pot and add the water. Cover and cook over low heat until the shells open, about 15 minutes. Do not overcook.

Put the clams in a large soup plate with a dish of melted butter on the side. Strain the broth into another dish. Lift each clam from the shell by its black neck, dip first in the broth and then in the butter and eat all but the neck.

Boiled Lobster

Hot or cold, lobster makes a wonderful solitary feast. The size of the lobster is up to you. Leftover lobster meat, combined with some diced celery and mayonnaise, makes a superb cold salad.

1 live lobster
Water
1 tablespoon salt
Melted butter for dipping or mayonnaise

Fill a large pot with water, and the salt and bring to a rapid boil. Put in the live lobster, grasping it just behind the claws. Bring the water to a boil again, then lower the heat, cover and simmer. Allow about 8–10 minutes for a small lobster, 10–15 minutes for a medium-sized one, and 15–20 minutes for a very large one. Dip the hot lobster meat in melted butter. If you prefer it cold, eat it with mayonnaise.

Broiled Lobster

Ask your fish dealer to prepare the lobster for broiling; he will cut it so that it will lie flat, and he will remove the intestinal vein and stomach. Have him do this as close to cooking time as possible, since you want the lobster to be very fresh.

1 lobster, prepared for broiling
Melted butter

Spread the lobster as flat as possible on its back and brush the meaty parts with melted butter. Place, still shell side down, on a broiler rack and broil slowly for 20 minutes, or until delicately browned. Dip in melted butter as you eat it.

Steamed Mussels

12 mussels in shells
2 stalks celery, diced
1 onion, sliced
2 tablespoons chopped parsley
1 clove garlic, peeled
½ lemon, sliced
½ cup water

Scrub the mussels and wash them in lukewarm water, changing the water at least three times.

Put the celery, onion, parsley, garlic, lemon and water in a deep pot and cook, covered, for 10 minutes until the vegetables are soft. Add the mussels, cover and steam for about 15 minutes, or until all the mussels are open. Discard unopened mussels. Spoon the mussels and pour the broth into a deep bowl and eat at once.

Oyster Pan Roast

Use the oyster juice in a fish soup or chowder.

2 tablespoons butter
½ cup shucked oysters, drained
Salt
Freshly ground pepper
Cayenne
1 slice toast
Chopped parsley
Lemon wedge

Heat the butter in a small skillet until bubbly. Add the oysters, cover and poach for 4–5 minutes, or until the edges curl and the oysters are plump. Season with salt, pepper and cayenne. Spoon over the toast, sprinkle with parsley and garnish with a wedge of lemon.

Sautéed Scallops with Lemon Butter

¼–½ pound scallops
Bread crumbs
1 tablespoon butter
Salt
Freshly ground pepper
Paprika
1 teaspoon chopped parsley
1 tablespoon lemon juice

Roll the scallops in the bread crumbs. Melt 1½ teaspoons of the butter in a skillet. Add the scallops and sauté slowly for 8 minutes, or until golden brown. Season with salt, pepper and paprika and turn gently to brown evenly. Remove the scallops to a hot plate. Put the remaining 1½ teaspoons of butter in the skillet and heat˙with the parsley and lemon juice. Pour over the scallops and eat immediately.

Scallops en Brochette

Three special ingredients combine to make this a splendid dish.

¼–½ pound scallops
6 whole mushrooms
2 slices bacon, in squares
Vinaigrette Dressing (p. 203)

Place the scallops, mushrooms and bacon squares alternately on a skewer. Grill over charcoal or under the broiler for about 10 minutes, brushing frequently with vinaigrette dressing.

Butterfly Shrimp

Jumbo shrimp are very costly—out of reach when there are many mouths to feed, but not when there's only one.

¼ pound raw jumbo shrimp
1 teaspoon flour
1½ teaspoons cornstarch
1½ teaspoons white cornmeal
¼ teaspoon baking powder
¼ teaspoon salt
3 tablespoons milk
Oil for deep-frying
Chinese Barbecue Sauce (p. 198)

Peel the shrimp, but leave the tails on. Make a deep slit along the back to "butterfly" the shrimp, removing the black vein as you do.

Mix the flour, cornstarch, cornmeal, baking powder and salt. Beat in the milk to make a thin batter. Dip each shrimp in the batter and fry in hot deep oil (375° on a frying thermometer) until golden brown, 2 or 3 minutes. Eat with Chinese barbecue sauce.

Shrimp Cooked in Beer

No need for a special sauce when you cook shrimp this way.

3 cups stale beer
1 cup water
1 teaspoon salt
2 peppercorns
1 small bay leaf
Sprinkling of celery seed
¼–½ pound shrimp, shelled and deveined

Put the beer and water in a pot and add the salt, peppercorns, bay leaf and celery seed. Bring to a boil, then add the shrimp and simmer, covered, for 2–5 minutes, until pink. Eat hot or cold.

Grilled Scampi, Venetian Style

Shell the shrimp if you are grilling them in the broiler. If you are lucky enough to be able to cook them over a charcoal fire, leave the shells on, but split them on the underside down to the tail, using a scissors or sharp knife and taking care not to cut the meat.

¼–½ pound raw jumbo shrimp (see above)
½ clove garlic, minced
Freshly ground black pepper
1 teaspoon lime juice
1 tablespoon olive oil
Garlic-Butter Dip (p. 198)

Put the shrimp in a bowl and add the garlic, pepper, lime juice and olive oil. Stir well to coat the shrimp, cover and refrigerate for at least 2 hours.

Put the shrimp on skewers and grill in the broiler or over slow charcoal fire, turning frequently, for about 15 minutes, or until done. Use the garlic-butter dip with each shrimp when you eat it.

VEGETABLES

✿➤

FROZEN VEGETABLES USUALLY COME IN PORTIONS too large for one person, though if you buy them in bags, you can easily separate what you need. Canned vegetables *do* come in small cans. Use fresh vegetables in season. They are readily available and in good variety in most parts of the country. Since most vegetables don't improve with age, buy only the amount you need.

Like the Chinese (and perhaps from them), Americans have learned in recent years not to overcook vegetables. Many traditionally boring vegetable dishes are wonderfully transformed when the vegetables are allowed to remain crisp-tender and thus to retain both their texture and flavor.

Green Beans in Herb Butter

You can cook these ahead, if convenient, and heat them in the herb butter just before eating.

¼ pound green beans, cut in 2-inch lengths
2 tablespoons minced onion
1 tablespoon butter
2 teaspoons minced parsley
1 teaspoon thyme, preferably fresh
2 teaspoons lemon juice
Salt
Freshly ground pepper
Dash of paprika

Bring a large pot of water to a boil, drop in the beans and cook them just until they are barely tender; test by tasting one. Remove the beans from the pot, plunge them into cold water to stop the cooking, then drain and set aside.

Cook the onion in the butter until tender, then add the parsley, thyme, lemon juice, salt, pepper and paprika and mix well. When you are ready to eat, heat the beans quickly in the herb butter.

Bean Sprouts with Green Pepper

A quick and unusual Chinese vegetable dish.

¼ pound fresh bean sprouts
1 green pepper, seeded and sliced the size of bean sprouts
1 tablespoon oil
2 teaspoons sherry
¼ teaspoon salt

Sauté the bean sprouts and green pepper in hot oil for 3 minutes. Add the sherry and salt, toss well and eat immediately.

Buttered Beets

Use small, tender new beets, if you can get them.

¼ pound small beets
Salt
Freshly ground pepper
About 1 tablespoon butter
Chopped parsley

Wash the beets and cut off the tops. Cook them, covered, in gently boiling water until they are tender when pierced with a fork, about 50 minutes to 1 hour. Let the cooked beets cool slightly, then slip off the skins and slice them. Put them in a small pan, season with salt and pepper, then add the butter and heat slowly until the butter has melted and the beets are hot. Sprinkle with parsley before eating.

Cabbage Sauté

¾ cup shredded cabbage
½ green pepper, in strips
2 teaspoons oil
¼ teaspoon cornstarch
2 teaspoons lemon juice
Salt
¼ teaspoon caraway seed

Sauté the cabbage and green pepper in hot oil until the cabbage begins to get tender. Mix the cornstarch with 2 tablespoons of cold water, then stir in the lemon juice, salt and caraway seed. Add to the skillet, and cook and stir until the vegetables are crisp-tender.

Mustard Carrots

2 tablespoons minced onion
2 teaspoons butter
¼ cup water
Salt
Freshly ground pepper
¾ cup sliced carrots, ¼-inch thick
2 tablespoons half-and-half
1 teaspoon flour
1 teaspoon prepared mustard

Sauté the onion in the butter until tender. Add the water, salt and pepper and bring to a boil. Put in the carrots, cover and simmer for about 8 minutes, until barely crisp-tender. Mix the half-and-half, flour and mustard together well. Blend into the carrots and cook, stirring, until slightly thickened.

Braised Celery with Peanut Sauce

¾ cup sliced celery
½ onion, sliced
1 tablespoon peanut butter
1½ teaspoons soy sauce

Put the celery, onion and 1 tablespoon of water in a small saucepan, bring to a boil, then cover and simmer for 5–8 minutes. Drain, reserving the liquid. Put the vegetables in a warm dish and return the liquid to the saucepan. Stir in the peanut butter and soy sauce. Add a little water if necessary, to thin the sauce, then heat and pour over the celery.

French Peas

Tender fresh spring peas are best, of course.

1 teaspoon butter
¼ cup thinly sliced mushrooms
½ cup shelled peas
2 thin slices onion
Salt

Melt the butter in a small saucepan, then add 2 teaspoons of water and the mushrooms, peas, onion and salt. Cover the pan tightly and cook until the peas are just tender, shaking occasionally and adding more water only if necessary.

Green-Pepper and Onion Skillet

1 small onion, thinly sliced
1 small green pepper, in strips
½ clove garlic, minced
1½ tablespoons olive oil
Pinch of oregano or basil
Salt
Freshly ground pepper

Sauté the onion, green pepper and garlic in hot oil for 1 or 2 minutes. Season to taste with oregano or basil, salt and pepper, cover and steam over low heat for 5–10 minutes, until crisp-tender.

Sautéed Mushrooms

1 tablespoon butter
¼ pound mushrooms, sliced
½ teaspoon lemon juice
Salt
Freshly ground pepper
Pinch of oregano

Melt the butter in a small skillet. Add the mushrooms and lemon juice and sauté over medium heat for 3–5 minutes, or until just tender. Season to taste with salt, pepper and oregano.

Mushrooms in Sour Cream

¼ pound mushrooms, sliced
1 teaspoon butter
2 tablespoons sour cream
1 teaspoon flour
Salt
Freshly ground pepper
2 tablespoons freshly grated Parmesan cheese
1 tablespoon chopped parsley

Preheat the oven to 425°.

Sauté the mushrooms quickly in butter until lightly browned. Blend the sour cream, flour, salt and pepper together, stir into the mushrooms and heat to just below the boiling point. Put in a small baking dish, sprinkle with the cheese and parsley, and bake for about 10 minutes.

Stuffed Potato

1 large Idaho potato
Salt
Freshly ground pepper
Paprika
About 1 tablespoon sour cream
1 teaspoon minced green onion

Scrub the potato and bake it in a 450° oven or toaster oven until tender, about 45–60 minutes. Slice an oval piece of skin from the top and scoop out the potato from the shell. Mash with salt, pepper and paprika, then add the sour cream and minced green onion. Fill the shell lightly with this mixture, return it to the hot oven and bake until lightly browned.

Potato Pancakes

Grating potatoes can be a nuisance when you need large quantities, but it's a snap to do for one.

½ cup grated potatoes
1 egg, well beaten
1½ teaspoons flour
¼ teaspoon salt
1 teaspoon grated onion
Oil for frying

Squeeze the grated potatoes as dry as possible. Combine them with the egg, flour, salt and onion, mixing well. Heat the oil in a small skillet. Pat the potato mixture into 3 or 4 flat patties and fry in hot oil, browning first one side and then the other. Eat immediately, while they are still very crisp.

Italian Spinach

Use any extra spinach in Egg-Spinach Salad (p.170).

¼–½ pound fresh spinach
1 tablespoon olive oil
1 small clove garlic, minced
Salt
Freshly ground pepper

Wash the spinach well and shake off the water. Heat the olive oil in a small skillet, add the garlic and sauté for a few minutes without letting the garlic brown. Add the spinach, cover and simmer until tender, about 6–8 minutes. Season to taste with salt and pepper.

Succotash

Make this with leftover vegetables, or with frozen vegetables if you wish.

¼ cup cooked corn
¼ cup cooked lima beans
1½ teaspoons butter
Salt
Freshly ground pepper

Combine all the ingredients in a small pan and heat slowly over very low heat.

Broiled Tomato

1 ripe tomato, halved
1 teaspoon sugar
Salt
Freshly ground pepper
½ teaspoon chopped fresh or dried basil
1 tablespoon minced onion
Bread crumbs
Butter

Place the tomato halves, cut side up, in a small pan. Mix together the sugar, salt, pepper, basil and onion and sprinkle over the tomato halves. Sprinkle lightly with bread crumbs and dot with butter. Broil until lightly browned on top.

Tomato Hash

2 tablespoons chopped onion
1½ slices firm bread, crumbled
1½ tablespoons butter
1 large tomato, peeled, cored and chopped
¼ teaspoon salt
Freshly ground pepper
Pinch of sage
Chopped parsley or chives

Sauté the onion and the crumbs in the butter until well browned. Add the tomato and mix lightly but thoroughly over medium heat. Season to taste with salt, pepper and sage. Sprinkle with parsley or chives before eating.

Pickled Turnips

Cool and crisp, a Chinese specialty.

1 small white turnip
1½ teaspoons salt
¼ cup vinegar
3 tablespoons sugar
Dash of paprika

Peel the turnip and cut it crosswise in thin slices no more than ¼-inch thick. Mix with the salt and let stand for an hour; drain. Bring the vinegar, sugar and paprika to a boil, add the turnip slices and simmer for 2 minutes. Let cool before eating.

Zucchini Pancakes

3 tablespoons flour
½ cup shredded zucchini
¼ teaspoon salt
Freshly ground pepper
1 egg, separated
Oil

Mix the flour, zucchini, salt, pepper and egg yolk in a small bowl. Beat the egg white in another bowl until stiff but not dry; fold into the zucchini mixture. Drop by heaping tablespoonfuls into hot oil in a skillet and brown on both sides.

Sautéed Zucchini

½ small onion, sliced thin
1 small zucchini, sliced thin
1 tablespoon butter
Salt
Freshly ground pepper

Sauté the onion and zucchini in the butter just until crisp-tender and golden. Season to taste with salt and pepper.

SALADS

THESE SALADS ARE EASY when you're cooking for one. Most of them are assembled from ingredients that are readily at hand, and many can be prepared in advance and kept in the refrigerator until needed.

A few of these salads are meant to accompany a meat or fish dish, but most of them are complete meals in themselves. A cold salad is the perfect lunch or dinner for a humid summer day, of course, but team it up with a bowl of steaming soup and you will have fine winter fare as well.

Pickled Cucumbers

This is a refreshing dish, nice with all kinds of meats, fish and poultry.

1 small cucumber, sliced thin
1 teaspoon salt
2 tablespoons vinegar
2 tablespoons sugar
½ teaspoon minced fresh gingerroot
½ teaspoon sesame seed

Mix the cucumber and salt in a bowl and let stand for 1 hour. Wrap in a thin clean towel and squeeze out the excess moisture. Mix the vinegar, sugar, gingerroot and sesame seed in a small pot and bring to a boil. Pour over the cucumber slices and chill.

Piquant Macaroni Salad

You can turn this into your main course by adding another ounce or so of macaroni and some sliced pepperoni or other cooked sausage.

2 ounces (½ cup) small elbow macaroni, cooked and
  rinsed
1 tablespoon chopped green onion
2 tablespoons sliced radishes
2 tablespoons chopped green pepper
2 tablespoons sliced celery
2 tablespoons mayonnaise
1 teaspoon prepared mustard
¼ teaspoon prepared horseradish
Salt
Freshly ground pepper

Toss the macaroni with the onion, radishes, green pepper
and celery. Mix together the mayonnaise, mustard and
horseradish, combine with the macaroni and toss again.
Season to taste with salt and pepper and chill before
eating.

Chef's Salad

*You can add any cooked leftover meat to this salad and
adjust the amounts according to how hungry you are.*

1 cup lettuce, in bite-sized pieces
¼–½ cup cooked ham, cut in julienne strips
¼ cup Swiss cheese, cut in julienne strips
2 tablespoons diced green pepper
2 tablespoons sliced pitted black olives
1 small pimiento, chopped
Chopped parsley
2–3 tablespoons Vinaigrette Dressing (p. 203)

Combine all the ingredients in a salad bowl, adding the dressing last. Toss gently and eat at once with a hot buttered biscuit or two to go with it.

Easy Chicken Salad

⅔ cup diced cooked chicken
2 tablespoons finely chopped celery
1 tablespoon Vinaigrette Dressing (p. 203)
1 tablespoon mayonnaise
Pinch of cayenne
Salt
Salad greens
Tomato wedges

Toss together the chicken, celery, vinaigrette dressing, mayonnaise and cayenne. Add salt, if necessary. Arrange on salad greens and garnish with tomato wedges.

Chicken-Grape Salad

⅔ cup diced cooked chicken
¼ cup sliced celery
1 tablespoon Vinaigrette Dressing (p. 203)
½ cup seedless grapes, halved
Salt
Freshly ground pepper
Salad greens
1 tablespoon mayonnaise
1 tablespoon sour cream
1 tablespoon toasted slivered almonds

Toss the chicken and celery in the vinaigrette dressing and let marinate for 1 hour. Add the grapes and season to taste with salt and pepper. Arrange on some salad greens on a plate. Mix the mayonnaise and sour cream and spoon on top of the chicken salad. Sprinkle with the almonds.

Green-Onion and Potato Salad

Try this with Cheese-Topped Frankfurters in Rolls (p. 59).

1 large potato
1 tablespoon salad oil
1 tablespoon wine vinegar
1 tablespoon water
1 tablespoon minced green onion
½ pimiento, minced
¼ teaspoon salt
Dash of paprika
Pinch of freshly ground pepper

Cook the potato in boiling water until just tender. While the potato is cooking, whisk together the rest of the ingredients. When the potato is cooked and still hot, peel and slice it and toss it in the dressing. Let it cool while you prepare the frankfurters.

Potato Salad, Hungarian Style

½ cup diced cooked potato
1 tablespoon diced peeled cucumber
1 tablespoon diced radishes
1 tablespoon chopped green onion
1 hard-cooked egg
Pinch of dry mustard
2 tablespoons sour cream
Dash of paprika
½ teaspoon cider vinegar
Scant ¼ teaspoon salt
Pinch of celery seed and/or poppy seed

Combine the potato, cucumber, radishes and green onion in a bowl; set aside. Separate the egg yolk from the white. Dice the white and add it to the vegetable mixture. Mash the yolk with the mustard and sour cream, then add the rest of the ingredients. Add the vegetables and mix well. Chill thoroughly. Adjust the seasonings before eating.

Italian-Style Potato Salad

½ cup diced cooked potato
2 teaspoons minced green onion
¼ cup diced unpeeled zucchini
2 ounces fresh mushrooms, sliced
½ small tomato, diced
1½ tablespoons olive oil
1 teaspoon lemon juice
¼ teaspoon basil leaves
⅛ teaspoon salt
Pinch of garlic powder
Pinch of oregano
Coarsely ground black pepper
2 teaspoons pine nuts

Combine the potato, onion, zucchini, mushrooms and tomato in a bowl; set aside. Mix together the olive oil, lemon juice, basil, salt, garlic powder, oregano and pepper. Pour over the vegetables, mix well and chill. Adjust the seasonings and sprinkle with nuts before eating.

Cold Salmon Platter

1 can (3¾ ounces) salmon, drained
¼ cup mayonnaise
1 teaspoon lemon juice
⅛ teaspoon prepared mustard
½ cucumber, peeled and sliced
1 small tomato, in wedges
1 hard-cooked egg, quartered
1 teaspoon chopped fresh dill
Salt
Freshly ground pepper

Separate the salmon into chunks and put them in the center of a plate. Mix together the mayonnaise, lemon juice and mustard and spread on the salmon. Arrange the cucumber, tomato and egg around the salmon. Sprinkle dill over the plate and season lightly with salt and pepper. Eat with buttered toast triangles if you wish.

Marinated Salmon Salad

1 can (3¾ ounces) salmon, drained
⅓ cup sour cream
¼ teaspoon salt
2 teaspoons lemon juice
2 tablespoons minced red onion
½ red onion, sliced thin
2 tablespoons minced green onion
1 tablespoon chopped parsley
2 whole allspice, bruised

Separate the salmon into chunks in a bowl. Mix together the sour cream, salt, lemon juice and minced red onion and pour over the salmon. Garnish with red onion slices. Combine the green onion and parsley and sprinkle over all. Sprinkle lightly with allspice and chill for at least 1 hour. Eat with wheat crackers or pumpernickel bread if you wish.

Sardine-Onion-Egg Platter

This couldn't be prettier or simpler to prepare, great for an impromptu lunch or casual dinner for one.

Salad greens
1 can (2½ ounces) boneless and skinless sardines, drained
½ sweet onion, sliced thin
1 small tomato, sliced
1 hard-cooked egg, quartered
Salt
Freshly ground pepper
Chopped parsley
¼ cup mayonnaise
1½ teaspoons prepared mustard
1½ teaspoons lemon juice
2 lemon wedges
Toasted rye bread

Arrange the salad greens on a plate and top them with the sardines, onion, tomato and egg. Sprinkle lightly with salt, pepper and parsley. Mix together the mayonnaise, mustard and lemon juice and use as a dressing on the side. Garnish the plate with the lemon wedges and toasted rye bread.

Tuna-Stuffed Tomato

1 large tomato
Salt
1 can (3½ ounces) tuna, drained and flaked
1 tablespoon minced onion
2 tablespoons minced celery
Freshly ground pepper
2 tablespoons sliced green olives
1½ tablespoons mayonnaise
Celery leaf
Curly endive

Cut a thin slice from the top of the tomato and scoop out the pulp. Sprinkle inside with salt and turn upside down to drain.

Combine the tuna with the onion, minced celery, pepper, olives and mayonnaise. Add a little of the tomato pulp, squeezed dry, if you wish, and season to taste with salt. Fill the tomato with the tuna mixture, top with a perky celery leaf and garnish the plate with endive.

West Coast Salad

A hot dressing of vinegar and bacon fat makes this special.

1½ cups packed, coarsely torn romaine lettuce leaves
1 hard-cooked egg, chopped
2 green onions, sliced thin
1 can (3½ ounces) tuna, drained and broken up
2 slices bacon
1 or more tablespoons wine vinegar
Freshly ground pepper
Salt

Put the romaine in a bowl and add the egg, onions and tuna. Fry the bacon until crisp; drain and break into the salad, reserving the fat. Add the vinegar to the bacon fat in the pan, together with a few grindings of pepper. Heat and pour over the salad. Sprinkle lightly with salt and mix gently.

Egg-Spinach Salad

Add another slice or two of bacon if you're very hungry.

1½ cups (about 3 ounces) packed, coarsely torn spinach
1 hard-cooked egg, sliced
3 tablespoons mayonnaise
1½ tablespoons chili sauce
1 teaspoon grated onion
2 slices bacon, fried crisp and crumbled
Garlic croutons

Put the spinach in a bowl and arrange the sliced egg on top. Mix together the mayonnaise, chili sauce and onion. Pour over the spinach and egg, toss lightly and sprinkle with the bacon and croutons.

Kidney-Bean and Egg Salad

Make this for lunch, or let it follow a bowl of hot soup for a satisfying dinner for one.

1 or 2 hard-cooked eggs
1 can (8¾ ounces) red kidney beans, drained
¼ cup chopped nuts
2 tablespoons sliced pitted black olives
1 green onion, minced
1½ tablespoons mayonnaise
2 teaspoons milk
Pinch of prepared mustard
Salt
Freshly ground pepper
Salad greens

Separate the egg yolk from the white. Crumble the yolk and set aside. Cut up the white and toss it lightly in a bowl with the beans, nuts, olives and green onion. Chill for at least 30 minutes. Blend the mayonnaise, milk and mustard, spoon over the egg-bean mixture and toss lightly. Season to taste with salt and pepper.

When ready to serve, line a small bowl with salad greens, fill with the salad and sprinkle with the crumbled egg yolk. Try this with a crusty garlic-buttered "hero" roll.

Chickpea, Salami and Cheese Platter

Although there's no one to see it but you, take a little extra time to arrange this salad platter attractively. Food tastes better when it is appealing to the eye.

1 can (10½ ounces) chickpeas, drained
2 tablespoons oil
2 tablespoons vinegar
1 small clove garlic, split
Salt
Freshly ground pepper
2–3 green onions, chopped
1 rib celery, in ½-inch pieces
Salad greens
3 thin slices salami
2–3 slices Swiss or provolone cheese
1 hard-cooked egg, halved
1 pimiento, halved
Paprika

Gently toss the chickpeas with the oil, vinegar, garlic, salt and pepper, and marinate for several hours; discard the garlic. Stir in the green onions and celery.

Arrange the salad greens on a plate and mound the chickpea salad in the center. Place slices of salami, cheese, egg and pimiento around the edges and sprinkle the egg with paprika. Eat with a warm roll.

Zucchini Salad

This delicious cold vegetable can be prepared a day ahead. It is good with any kind of meat dish, especially with lamb.

1 medium zucchini, sliced thin
2 green onions with tops, sliced thin
3 tablespoons oil
1 tablespoon wine vinegar
½ small clove garlic, minced
Salt
Freshly ground pepper

Put the zucchini and onions in a bowl. Mix together the rest of the ingredients, pour over the zucchini and toss. Cover and chill for at least 1 hour.

RICE
and PASTA

❀⟩

RICE AND PASTA ARE INEXPENSIVE STAPLES, readily at hand and easy to measure out in small quantities. In addition, really good rice and pasta dishes are usually simple to prepare.

The rice recipes in this section, with the possible exception of Pork Fried Rice, are intended as side dishes to be eaten along with vegetables and meat; if you want to turn them into main courses, you should add some leftover diced meat and vegetables. The noodle and spaghetti recipes in this chapter, with the exception of Noodles Polonaise, are intended as main courses.

Try to balance rice and pasta main courses with protein, a nourishing soup or a fresh green salad. Rice and pasta are good enough to eat every day, but as a steady diet they will not provide the balanced nutrition that we all need.

Substitute brown rice or various shapes of pasta in these recipes if you wish. Note that brown rice will take longer to cook than white.

It is important to taste rice and pasta frequently during cooking to determine exactly when they are done: over-cooked pasta or rice will be soft and gluey. Pasta should always be cooked *al dente*—to the point where it offers some resistance to the teeth. Rice should be dry and fluffy, or have moist, separated grains.

Cook pasta by putting it into a large amount of boiling salted water, and be sure to keep the water boiling throughout the cooking. If spaghetti is too long to fit into the pot, do not break it: stand it upright in the pot until the submerged ends soften enough to bend. Stir spaghetti from time to time during cooking to keep it from sticking together. Drain it in a colander the moment it is just tender. If you must hold spaghetti for a while before eating it, toss it with some butter or oil or a little bit of the sauce to keep the strands separate.

Rice should be stirred at the beginning of cooking and then left alone. If you are adding liquid to rice while it is cooking, be sure that it is boiling hot, When simmering rice in a pilaf dish, keep the lid on tight and do not stir until all the liquid has been absorbed. Never wash rice before or after cooking, or you will rinse away valuable nutrients.

Mushroom Rice

1 scallion, chopped
4–6 mushrooms, sliced
1 tablespoon butter
¼ cup uncooked rice
½ cup beef bouillon
¼ teaspoon soy sauce

Sauté the scallion and mushrooms in hot butter until tender, add the rice and sauté, stirring, for about 5 minutes. Stir in the bouillon and the soy sauce, cover the pot and simmer until the liquid is absorbed, about 20–25 minutes. Let stand for 5 minutes, uncovered, before eating.

Yellow Rice

¼ cup uncooked rice
½ cup boiling water
¼ teaspoon salt
¼ teaspoon turmeric
2 teaspoons butter

Preheat the oven to 350°.

Combine all the ingredients in a small casserole, cover and bake for 1½ hours or a little more, until the rice is tender.

Brown-Rice Pilaf

Brown rice takes longer to cook than white rice.

2 green onions, chopped
2 teaspoons butter
4–5 mushrooms, chopped
¼ cup brown rice
¾ cup boiling water
1 bouillon cube
Minced parsley

Sauté the onions in the butter until tender but not browned. Add the mushrooms and sauté for another 2 or 3 minutes. Add the rice and cook over low heat 2 or 3 minutes more, stirring, until the rice is translucent. Add the boiling water and bouillon cube, bring to a boil, stir, then cover and steam over very low heat without stirring for about 45 minutes, or until the rice is tender and the liquid absorbed. Uncover, fluff with a fork, and let dry over low heat for a few minutes. Sprinkle with parsley before eating.

Herb Pilaf

Fresh herbs are preferable to dried ones. Use them if you can get hold of them, but double the amount for each herb.

¼ cup uncooked rice
1 tablespoon minced green onion
1 tablespoon butter
¼ teaspoon salt
Freshly ground pepper
⅛ teaspoon dried tarragon
⅛ teaspoon dried thyme
⅛ teaspoon dried basil
⅛ teaspoon minced parsley
½ cup beef bouillon

Sauté the rice and the green onion in the butter, stirring frequently, until the rice is translucent. Season with the salt, pepper, tarragon, thyme, basil and parsley, cooking for a minute or two until well combined. Add the bouillon, bring to a boil, then cover and simmer without stirring until the rice is tender and the liquid absorbed.

Pork Fried Rice

This is a flexible recipe, designed to help you use up bits and pieces of leftovers in your refrigerator. It's good with any Chinese-style meat or poultry dish, or add a little more meat and vegetables to the rice and you will have a complete dinner for one. Ham, chicken, beef, shrimp or crab meat may be substituted for the pork.

1 tablespoon diced green onion
1–2 tablespoons peanut oil
¼ cup diced cooked pork
¼ cup diced cooked vegetables (peas, beans, broccoli, bean sprouts, etc.)
1 cup cold cooked rice
1 egg, beaten
2 teaspoons soy sauce

Sauté the green onion in the oil until tender. Add the pork, vegetables and rice and stir-fry until heated through. Add the egg and the soy sauce and cook a few minutes more, tasting and adjusting the seasonings. Eat at once.

Cheese Risotto

¼ cup chopped onion
1 tablespoon butter
¼ cup uncooked rice
4 ounces canned tomatoes and juice
1 chicken bouillon cube
¼ cup shredded sharp Cheddar cheese

Cook the onion in the butter until tender. Add the rice and cook, stirring, until very lightly browned. Add the tomatoes in their juice and the bouillon cube, bring to a boil and stir until the bouillon cube has dissolved. Cover and simmer for 20–25 minutes, or until the liquid is absorbed, adding a little boiling water only if the rice is not done when the liquid is gone. Stir the cheese in gently until it melts and eat immediately.

Macaroni-Chicken-Cheese Casserole

2–3 ounces elbow macaroni, cooked and drained
½ cup sliced, cooked chicken
2 ounces sliced American cheese
1 tablespoon butter
2 teaspoons flour
½ cup milk
Salt
Freshly ground pepper

Preheat the oven to 375°.

Put the macaroni in a small baking dish. Top it with the chicken and then with the cheese.

Melt the butter in a small pan, then stir in the flour and cook over low heat, stirring, for about 2 minutes. Add the milk and cook, stirring, until thickened. Season to taste with salt and pepper and pour the sauce over the mixture in the dish. Bake for 25–30 minutes.

Cottage-Cheese Noodles

A quick dinner when starting from scratch, or a good way to use up leftover cooked noodles.

2 tablespoons butter
2 tablespoons chopped green onion
2 ounces flat noodles, cooked and drained
4 ounces creamed cottage cheese
Salt
Freshly ground pepper

Melt the butter in a saucepan and sauté the onion in it until crisp-tender. Stir in the noodles and cottage cheese and heat through, seasoning with salt and pepper. Eat at once.

Noodles Polonaise

This is good with beef and pork dishes.

1 tablespoon butter
2 tablespoons fresh bread crumbs
1 hard-cooked egg, chopped
1 teaspoon chopped chives
⅛ teaspoon salt
2 ounces wide flat noodles, cooked and drained

Melt the butter in a small skillet, then add the crumbs and toast them lightly. Add the egg, chives and salt and mix well. Add the noodles, toss to coat them and heat through, stirring.

Spaghetti with White Clam Sauce

Keep a can of minced clams in your cupboard, and you can always have this lovely dish as a last-minute treat.

1 tablespoon olive oil
1 tablespoon minced green onion
2 sprigs parsley, chopped
1 small clove garlic, minced
4 ounces canned minced clams with juice
¼ teaspoon salt
Freshly ground pepper
¼ pound spaghetti

Heat the oil in a small skillet. Add the green onion, parsley and garlic and sauté for 2–3 minutes. Add the clams, salt and pepper and heat through. Cook the spaghetti in a separate pot of boiling salted water until it is just tender but still chewy. Drain it, then mix it with the hot sauce and eat at once.

Spaghetti with Herbs

Make this only with fresh *herbs.*

1 clove garlic, minced
2 teaspoons olive oil
2 tablespoons hot melted butter
¼ cup chopped mixed fresh herbs (chives, parsley, dill,
    marjoram, scallion tops)
Salt
¼ pound thin spaghetti

Sauté the garlic in the oil just until it begins to color.
Remove from the heat and add the hot melted butter and
the herbs. Sprinkle with salt and let steep while you prepare the spaghetti.

Cook the spaghetti in a large pot filled with boiling
salted water until the spaghetti is just tender but still
chewy. Drain, then toss in the herb sauce and eat immediately.

Spaghetti Carbonara

¼ pound spaghetti
2–3 strips bacon, cooked until crisp, and crumbled
1 egg, beaten
1 tablespoon butter
2–3 tablespoons freshly grated Parmesan cheese
Salt
Freshly ground pepper

Cook the spaghetti in boiling salted water until just tender; drain. Return the spaghetti to the pot and add the rest of the ingredients. Cook over low heat, tossing gently, for a few minutes until the egg begins to thicken.

Spaghetti with Olive Oil and Garlic

The simplest spaghetti sauce of all, and quite possibly the best.

1 clove garlic, minced
2 teaspoons butter
1 tablespoon olive oil
¼ pound spaghetti
2 tablespoons freshly grated Parmesan cheese
Salt
Freshly ground pepper

Sauté the garlic in hot butter and oil until golden; remove from the heat. Cook the spaghetti in boiling salted water until just tender; drain. Return to the pot and toss with the garlic mixture, adding the Parmesan and some salt and pepper to taste.

Spaghetti with Fresh Tomato Sauce

1 clove garlic, minced
1 tablespoon olive oil
½ pound fresh tomatoes, peeled and chopped
Salt
Freshly ground pepper
1 tablespoon chopped parsley
¼ pound spaghetti
Freshly grated Parmesan cheese

Sauté the garlic in the oil until soft but not browned. Add the tomatoes, salt, pepper and parsley and simmer, uncovered, for about 30 minutes. Adjust the seasonings.

Cook the spaghetti in boiling salted water until just tender; drain. Return to the pot, toss with the sauce and eat at once, sprinkling with freshly grated Parmesan cheese.

Spaghetti with Tuna Sauce

Add a few coarsely chopped black olives to this if you have some.

1 small clove garlic, minced
2 tablespoons finely chopped onion
1 tablespoon olive oil
1 can (3½ ounces) tuna in oil
¼ cup hot water
2 ounces tomato paste
2 tablespoons white wine
Salt
Freshly ground pepper
1 tablespoon minced parsley
¼ pound spaghettini
Freshly grated Parmesan cheese

Sauté the garlic and onion in oil until soft. Put the tuna in a strainer over the pan and pour the hot water over it; reserve the tuna. Add the tomato paste and wine to the pan and simmer for about 20 minutes, seasoning to taste with salt and pepper. Flake the tuna and add it and the parsley to the pan.

Cook the spaghettini in boiling salted water until just tender; drain. Pour the hot sauce over the spaghettini and toss well. Eat sprinkled with Parmesan cheese.

Fettucini alla Romana

Simple, rich and delicious. Use lots of pepper.

⅓ cup heavy cream
3 tablespoons butter
4 ounces fettucini noodles
Salt
3 ounces Parmesan cheese, freshly grated
Freshly ground pepper

Heat the cream and butter in a saucepan over very low heat. Cook the fettucini in boiling salted water until just tender; drain. Return the noodles to the pot, pour the cream-butter mixture over them, then add the Parmesan cheese, salt and pepper. Toss quickly over very low heat and eat immediately.

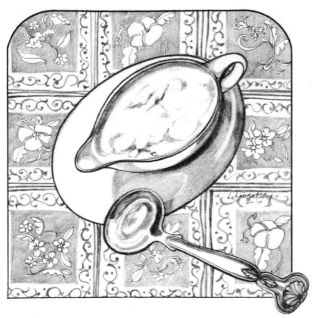

SAUCES
and DRESSINGS

✦)

✿❀✿❀✿❀✿❀✿❀✿❀✿❀✿❀✿❀✿❀✿❀✿❀✿❀✿❀✿❀✿❀

NO MATTER HOW WELL YOU PLAN or how carefully you follow a recipe for one, there are bound to be times when you find yourself with leftovers at hand. There may even be times when you intentionally cook more than you need for one meal in order to save cooking the next day. But who wants to eat leftovers in exactly the same form as they appeared the day before?

If you have a good repertoire of sauces and dressings to choose from, you will never be at a loss as to what to do with cooked or leftover food. This chapter contains recipes for hot and cold sauces and dressings that go with meat, fish, poultry, vegetables, salads, eggs and just about anything you may have, either freshly cooked or left over. Moreover, these sauces and dressings will not only help to refashion second-day food but also enhance your cooking in general, adding new zest and variety to plain foods or to overused recipes.

Hollandaise Sauce

This is essential to Eggs Benedict, of course. It's also great with vegetables such as broccoli and asparagus or with hot or cold poached fish.

1 egg yolk
Pinch of salt
Pinch of cayenne
1 teaspoon lemon juice
2½ tablespoons melted butter
1 tablespoon hot water

Beat the egg yolk in the top part of a small double boiler, then add the salt, cayenne and lemon juice. Stir in the butter and hot water. Place over hot, *not boiling*, water and cook, stirring, for 3 or 4 minutes, or until thickened. You will have about ¼ cup of sauce.

Béarnaise Sauce

Here's a Sauce Béarnaise that you can make in a blender. It is traditionally served with filet mignon, but it's good with all sorts of food.

2 teaspoons white wine
1 teaspoon tarragon vinegar
1 teaspoon chopped, fresh tarragon (or ½ teaspoon dried)
½ teaspoon finely chopped shallot or green onion
Freshly ground pepper
1 egg yolk
Pinch of salt
Pinch of cayenne
2½ tablespoons hot melted butter

In a small saucepan, combine the wine, vinegar, tarragon, shallot and pepper. Bring to a boil and cook rapidly until most of the liquid has disappeared. Put the egg yolk, salt, cayenne and the wine-tarragon mixture in a blender container. Cover and flick the motor on and off at high speed. Turn on to high and gradually add the hot butter until thick and smooth. You will have about ¼ cup of sauce.

Creamy Mushroom Sauce

This is good with any kind of meat, chicken or fish.

¼ pound chopped mushrooms
1 tablespoon butter
1 tablespoon flour
½ cup light cream
¼ teaspoon steak sauce
Salt
Freshly ground pepper
Sherry

Sauté the mushrooms in the butter for about 2 minutes. Stir in the flour and cook for about a minute or two more. Gradually add the cream and cook, stirring, until the sauce reaches the boiling point and thickens. Add the steak sauce and the salt, pepper and sherry to taste. You will have about ¾ cup of sauce.

Barbecue Sauce

It hardly pays to make a tiny amount of this barbecue sauce, since it will keep for several weeks in the refrigerator and can also be frozen. Use it when you broil chicken, steak or chops; you will have enough for about four meals.

1 can (8 ounces) tomato sauce
½ cup minced green onions
1 clove garlic, minced
½ cup chopped fresh mushrooms
2 tablespoons vegetable oil
1 tablespoon molasses
2 tablespoons vinegar
1 teaspoon steak sauce
1 teaspoon salt
½ teaspoon dry mustard
Dash of Tabasco sauce

Combine all of the ingredients. Cook over low heat, stirring occasionally, for about 15 minutes. Brush the meat frequently with the sauce when you broil it.

Sweet-and-Sour Sauce

Try this with ham or pork chops, or any leftover meat. If you can, cook it in the pan in which you've sautéed the meat, scraping the pan drippings into the sauce.

1½ teaspoons cider vinegar
½ teaspoon dry mustard
1½ teaspoons honey
¼ cup chili sauce
¼ cup golden raisins
1 tablespoon sherry
1 tablespoon water

Combine all the ingredients in a small pan and simmer for about 10 minutes. You will have about ½ cup of sauce.

Maître d'Hôtel Butter

Excellent with fish.

¼ cup butter
1½ teaspoons lemon juice
Salt
Freshly ground pepper
½ teaspoon minced parsley

Melt the butter, then stir in the lemon juice, salt, pepper and parsley.

Garlic-Butter Dip

Use this as a dip for Grilled Scampi, Venetian Style (p. 142).

¼ cup melted butter
½ teaspoon Worcestershire sauce
1½ teaspoons lemon juice
⅛ teaspoon Tabasco sauce
½ clove garlic, minced
Salt to taste

Heat all the ingredients in a small saucepan. Use the dip hot or at room temperature.

Chinese Barbecue Sauce

Use this as a dip for Butterfly Shrimp (p. 140).

2 tablespoons soy sauce
1 tablespoon honey
1 tablespoon sherry
¼ teaspoon salt
Freshly ground pepper
½ clove garlic, minced

Combine all the ingredients in a small saucepan and heat for about 5 minutes. Use hot.

Spicy Marinade

This is a fine marinade/sauce for any kind of skewered dish: beef, lamb or vegetables, or a combination of things.

2 tablespoons fresh lemon juice
3 tablespoons oil
½ onion, grated
1½ teaspoons salt
1½ teaspoons chili powder
1 teaspoon curry powder
1 small clove garlic, minced

Combine all the ingredients thoroughly. Add meat and/or vegetables, stir and refrigerate for several hours or over-night, stirring occasionally.

Drain the meat or vegetables and thread on skewers, reserving the marinade. Place under the broiler and broil about 5 inches from the heat, basting with the marinade, until done.

Russian Dressing

Russian dressing is good with salads, sandwiches, hard-cooked eggs and raw vegetables, among many other things. Keep it covered and refrigerated until you're ready to use it.

¼ cup mayonnaise
2 tablespoons chili sauce
1 tablespoon pickle relish

Mix the ingredients together thoroughly. You will have about ½ cup of dressing.

Tartar Sauce

Try this with Salmon Patties (p. 134) or any other kind of fish.

½ cup mayonnaise
½ teaspoon prepared mustard
1 tablespoon chopped dill pickle or pickle relish
1½ teaspoons chopped drained capers
1½ teaspoons minced parsley

Combine all the ingredients thoroughly. You will have about ½ cup of sauce.

Tuna Mayonnaise

A nice way to dress up any form of salad on a hot summer day, and a good way to use up some leftover tuna fish.

Try this sauce with hard-cooked eggs, sliced tomatoes, cold green beans, sliced cucumbers, salad greens or a combination of any of these.

½ cup mayonnaise
About 1 ounce tuna fish
½ anchovy (optional)

Put the mayonnaise into a blender container. Add the tuna, and some anchovy if you wish, and whirl until smooth.

Mustard-Dill Sauce

Try this with just about anything: salads, cold fish or chicken, or leftover vegetables. All the ingredients should be at room temperature before you mix them.

3 tablespoons prepared mustard
1 tablespoon sugar
1 tablespoon wine vinegar
3 tablespoons vegetable oil
¼ teaspoon salt
Freshly ground pepper
3 tablespoons finely chopped fresh dill

Put the mustard in a small mixing bowl, add the sugar and vinegar and mix well. Very gradually mix in the oil, stirring briskly until the sauce is thick and shiny. Season with salt and pepper, then stir in the dill. You will have about ½ cup of sauce; what's left over will keep in the refrigerator indefinitely.

Pimiento Vinaigrette Dressing

This is especially beautiful when tossed with dark-green spinach leaves.

¼ cup oil
2 tablespoons wine vinegar
Salt
Freshly ground pepper
1 pimiento, drained and sliced thin

Beat the oil, vinegar, salt and pepper together with a whisk. Stir in the pimiento. You will have about ½ cup of dressing.

Green French Dressing

Make this in a blender or food processor if you have one. If you want to beat it up by hand, use a whisk and mince the parsley first.

¼ cup oil
1 tablespoon wine vinegar
½ teaspoon prepared mustard
Salt
Freshly ground pepper
Pinch of cayenne
¼ cup chopped parsley

Put all the ingredients in a blender or food processor and whirl until well blended. You will have about ⅓ cup of dressing.

Vinaigrette Dressing

Simple and classic, a basic dressing for salads, cold vegetables, cold fish, chicken or leftovers.

¼ cup olive oil
2 tablespoons wine vinegar
Pinch of dry mustard
Salt
Freshly ground pepper

Beat the oil and vinegar together with a whisk. Season to taste with mustard, salt and pepper.

Tomato French Dressing

2 tablespoons chili sauce
¼ cup salad oil
2 tablespoons vinegar
½ teaspoon dry mustard
½ teaspoon salt
½ teaspoon Worcestershire sauce
Dash of hot-pepper sauce
1 small clove garlic, minced

Put all the ingredients in a jar, cover tightly and shake well. Chill for a few hours. Shake well again before using. You will have about ½ cup of dressing.

Cottage- and Blue-Cheese Dressing

½ cup creamed cottage cheese
1½ teaspoons lemon juice
1 teaspoon minced onion
2 tablespoons water
¼ cup crumbled blue cheese

Put the cottage cheese, lemon juice, minced onion and water in a blender container and whirl until smooth and creamy. Add the blue cheese and whirl a bit longer, until just blended. You will have about ¾ cup of dressing.

EGGS
and CRÊPES

꧁꧂꧁꧂꧁꧂꧁꧂꧁꧂꧁꧂꧁꧂꧁꧂꧁꧂꧁꧂꧁꧂꧁꧂꧁꧂꧁꧂꧁꧂꧁

❖❿❖❿❖❿❖❿❖❿❖❿❖❿❖❿❖❿❖❿❖❿❖❿❖❿❖❿❖❿❖❿❖❿❖❿❿

JUST A FEW SMALL TOUCHES can transform eggs and pancakes—those simple, last-minute, everyday foods—and take them from the breakfast room to the dining table. You will find that certain egg dishes are more suitable for one diner than for large groups—Eggs Benedict, for example, or special omelets are best made in individual servings, one at a time, and eaten immediately.

Although eggs will keep for a long time in the refrigerator, they do lose their fresh flavor. It is advisable to buy them by the half-dozen when you live alone.

Crêpes, unlike egg dishes, can be made in advance. It pays to make more than you need because they are so infinitely versatile.

Hearty Omelet

2 eggs, separated
2 tablespoons milk
¼ cup leftover mashed potato
Salt
Freshly ground pepper
1 teaspoon butter
¼ cup grated Cheddar cheese

Beat the egg yolks, then mix in the milk and potato. Season to taste with salt and pepper. In a separate bowl, beat the egg whites until stiff and fold them into the egg-yolk mixture.

Melt the butter in a skillet with a cover. Pour in the egg mixture, sprinkle with the cheese, cover and cook slowly until puffy on top and lightly browned on the bottom. Fold in half and eat at once.

Mushroom Omelet

¼ pound mushrooms, sliced thin
1 tablespoon butter
1 tablespoon water
Salt
Freshly ground pepper
Paprika
2 eggs

Sauté the mushrooms in 2 teaspoons of the butter for about 3–4 minutes; season with salt, pepper and paprika and set aside. Beat the eggs lightly with the water and season them with salt and pepper.

Heat the remaining teaspoon of butter in a small skillet. Pour in the eggs, let the edges set for a minute, then draw the edges toward the center with a fork, tilting the skillet so that the uncooked portion flows to the bottom. When the bottom is set and the surface is still moist, spoon the mushrooms over one half and fold the other half over them. Turn onto a plate and eat at once.

Salmon Omelet

2 eggs, slightly beaten
2 tablespoons milk
⅛ teaspoon salt
1 tablespoon chopped parsley
1 tablespoon minced green onion
1 can (3¾ ounces) salmon, drained and flaked
1½ teaspoons butter

Lightly mix together the eggs, milk, salt, parsley, green onion and salmon. Melt the butter in a small skillet over medium heat. Pour in the egg mixture, cover and cook until set but still creamy.

Sailor's Omelet

How to make a slice of smoked salmon go a long way.

1 clove garlic, peeled
1 tablespoon anchovy paste
1½ teaspoons heavy cream
2 eggs
2 teaspoons chopped parsley
Pinch of cayenne pepper
1½ teaspoons butter
1 slice smoked salmon

Rub a bowl with the garlic. Put the anchovy paste and the cream in the bowl and mix until smooth. Add the eggs, parsley and pepper and beat well.

Heat the butter in a small skillet. Pour in the egg mixture, let the edges set for a minute, then draw the edges toward the center with a fork, tilting the skillet so that the uncooked portion flows to the bottom. When the bottom is set and the top still slightly moist, fold the omelet. Turn onto a plate and garnish with the smoked salmon.

Salami and Eggs

2–3 slices salami, cubed
1½ teaspoons butter
2 eggs
Salt
Freshly ground pepper
1 tablespoon tomato juice

Brown the salami lightly in the butter. Beat the eggs with the salt, pepper and tomato juice. Pour over the salami and cook slowly, scrambling the eggs with a fork until. they are the consistency you like.

Chicken Livers, Potato and Eggs

1 slice bacon
¼ pound chicken livers
1 medium potato, sliced thin
Salt
Freshly ground pepper
2 eggs
1 tablespoon milk
1 tablespoon minced parsley

Fry the bacon until crisp; remove from the skillet and crumble. Sauté the chicken livers in the bacon fat until just cooked through; remove and keep warm. Add the potato to the bacon fat in the skillet, season with salt and pepper, cover and cook over low heat until tender.

Beat the eggs with the milk and season with salt and pepper. Pour over the potatoes and cook over low heat, stirring occasionally, until the eggs are set. Sprinkle with the parsley and the crumbled bacon and turn onto a plate with the sautéed chicken livers.

Piperade

A Basque specialty.

2 tablespoons chopped onion
2 tablespoons chopped green pepper
1 small clove garlic, minced
1 tablespoon olive oil
2 ounces stewed tomatoes
2 eggs, beaten
Salt
Freshly ground pepper
Parsley sprigs or watercress

Sauté the onion, green pepper and garlic in hot oil until tender. Add the tomatoes and simmer for 10–15 minutes, or until most of the liquid evaporates. Season the eggs with salt and pepper, add to the tomato mixture and cook over low heat, stirring gently, until set. Garnish with parsley or watercress and eat immediately.

Scrambled Eggs with Cheese

1 tablespoon chopped onion
1½ teaspoons butter
2 eggs
1 tablespoon water
3 tablespoons shredded Cheddar cheese
Salt
Freshly ground pepper

Sauté the onion in the butter until golden. Beat the eggs
with the water and add them and the cheese to the pan.
Cook over low heat, stirring gently, until the eggs are the
consistency you like. Season with salt and pepper and eat
at once.

Scrambled Eggs with Cream Cheese

2 eggs
2 tablespoons light cream
1 teaspoon chopped chives
Salt
Freshly ground pepper
1½ teaspoons butter
1-ounce slice cream cheese

Beat the eggs and cream together, then add the chives,
salt and pepper.

Heat the butter in a skillet, add the egg mixture and cook over low heat, stirring gently, just until it begins to set. Add the slice of cream cheese and cook until the cheese begins to melt but the eggs are still moist. Eat at once.

Eggs Benedict

This elegant dish is a bit of a production to prepare for many people at once, but it's easy to fix for just one. Save it for a private celebration—a tossed salad and a glass of red wine are the perfect accompaniments.

Hollandaise Sauce (p. 194)
2 thin slices ham
Butter
1 English muffin, split
2 eggs

Prepare the hollandaise sauce and set it aside over warm water.

Fry the ham slices in a little bit of butter until lightly browned; keep warm. Bring a pan of salted water to a boil. Butter and toast the English-muffin halves while you poach the eggs by slipping them carefully into the boiling water and letting them simmer until the whites have just set. Remove with slotted spoon.

Top each muffin half with a slice of ham and then with a poached egg. Spoon the hollandaise sauce over all and eat immediately.

Eggs à la Suisse

1 teaspoon butter
¼ cup heavy cream
2 eggs
Salt
Freshly ground pepper
Pinch of cayenne
2 tablespoons freshly grated Parmesan cheese
2 slices buttered toast
1–2 teaspoons sherry

Melt the butter in a skillet, then stir in the cream and heat. Break in the eggs, one at a time, and dust them with salt, pepper and cayenne. Cook over medium-low heat until the whites are almost set. Sprinkle with the grated cheese and cook until the whites are firm. Remove each egg to a slice of buttered toast. Stir the sherry into the cream in the pan and heat, stirring. Pour over the eggs and toast and eat at once.

Venetian Eggs

A simple, piquant sauce that will transform fried eggs from breakfast to dinner food.

½ sweet red pepper, chopped
1 small tomato, in chunks
1–2 anchovies, diced
Freshly ground pepper
Pinch of oregano
½ teaspoon olive oil
2 eggs
1½ teaspoons butter

Combine the red pepper, tomato, anchovies, pepper, oregano and olive oil in a small saucepan and simmer for about 10 minutes. Fry the eggs in butter. Pour the sauce over them and eat immediately.

Shirred Eggs with Ham

A package of sliced ham will keep for quite a while in your refrigerator. Use some in this recipe, and keep the remainder for dishes like Eggs Benedict (p. 214), Chef's Salad (p. 161), Chicken-Ham Rolls (p. 115), or instead of bologna in French-Toasted Bologna-Cheese Sandwich (p. 30).

2–3 tablespoons chopped, cooked ham
1 teaspoon butter
2 eggs
Salt
Freshly ground pepper
2 tablespoons heavy cream

Preheat the oven to 400°.

Sauté the ham in hot butter until lightly browned. Put in a individual ramekin or small baking dish. Break the eggs onto the ham, taking care to keep the yolks whole. Season with salt and pepper and add the cream. Bake for 10–15 minutes, or until done as you like them.

Egg-Stuffed Tomato

1 tomato
2 eggs
1 small clove garlic, minced
Chopped parsley
Salt
Freshly ground pepper
1 tablespoon grated sharp Cheddar cheese
1 tablespoon bread crumbs
2 teaspoons butter

Preheat the oven to 350°.

Cut the tomato in half and scrape out the center and most of the juice. Put the tomato shells in a small baking dish and bake for 10 minutes. Remove the baking dish

from the oven and break an egg into each tomato half.
Sprinkle a little garlic and parsley over each egg and
season with salt and pepper. Mix the cheese and crumbs
and sprinkle over each egg, dot with butter and bake at
425° for 15 minutes, or until the tops are golden and the
eggs have set.

Spanish Eggs and Rice

Use leftover rice if you have it.

¼ cup uncooked rice (or ¾ cup cooked rice)
2 eggs
5 ounces canned tomatoes
1 teaspoon minced onion
½ small bay leaf
1 whole clove
¼ teaspoon sugar
Freshly ground pepper
¼ teaspoon salt
¼ teaspoon celery seed
¼ teaspoon paprika
¼ teaspoon Worcestershire sauce
2 teaspoons butter
2 teaspoons flour
⅓ cup buttered bread crumbs
2 teaspoons freshly grated Parmesan cheese

Preheat the oven to 350°.

Cook the rice and drain it. Put it in a shallow baking dish. Make 2 indentations in the rice and break an egg into each.

Combine in a saucepan the tomatoes, onion, bay leaf, clove, sugar, pepper, salt, celery seed, paprika and Worcestershire sauce. Bring to a boil, then simmer for about 10 minutes.

Melt the butter in a small pan, then blend in the flour and cook over low heat, stirring, for 2 minutes. Strain the tomato mixture into the butter-flour mixture and cook, stirring, until thickened. Pour over the eggs and rice. Mix the crumbs and cheese together and sprinkle them over the contents of the baking dish. Bake for about 20 minutes.

Cuban Eggs

2 hard-cooked eggs
Salt
Freshly ground pepper
Pinch of dry mustard
1 teaspoon cream
¼ cup grated sharp Cheddar cheese
2 tablespoons minced onion
1 tablespoon minced green pepper
2 teaspoons butter
4 ounces tomato sauce
Hot cooked rice

Preheat the oven to 450°.

Cut the eggs in half lengthwise and remove the yolks. Mash the yolks in a bowl, adding the salt, pepper, mustard, cream and 2 tablespoons of the Cheddar cheese. Mix well, then stuff the whites with the mixture. Arrange the stuffed eggs in a shallow baking dish.

In a small pan, cook the onion and green pepper in the hot butter for about 5 minutes. Add the tomato sauce and heat well. Pour the sauce over the eggs and sprinkle with the remaining 2 tablespoons of cheese. Bake for about 15 minutes. Eat with rice.

Hard-Cooked Eggs and Potato

1 cup raw diced potato
½ cup boiling water
½ teaspoon salt
Freshly ground pepper
2 tablespoons minced onion
1 tablespoon butter
2 hard-cooked eggs, in chunks
1 tablespoon milk
Chopped parsley

Put the potato, boiling water and salt in a skillet. cover and cook for 10 minutes. Uncover and cook until the water has completely evaporated. Add the pepper, onion and butter and cook over low heat, stirring occasionally, until potato is tender and lightly browned. Add the eggs and milk and heat through. Sprinkle with the parsley before eating.

Crêpes

This recipe will make 8 crêpes, far more than you need for one meal. But you won't mind having some extra crêpes on hand, for they are an especially wonderful treat when you are dining alone.

Crêpes may be made ahead, stacked and frozen; they will also keep for a few days in the refrigerator, either filled or unfilled. Use simple leftovers to fill them or try one of the fillings suggested below. They also make a fine dessert, filled with jam and sprinkled with confectioners' sugar.

1 egg
Pinch of salt
½ cup flour
½ cup milk
1 tablespoon melted butter

Put all the ingredients in a blender and whirl for about 1 minute. Scrape the sides with a rubber spatula, then whirl for another 15 seconds, or until smooth. Cover and refrigerate for at least 1 hour.

When ready to cook, heat a 6-inch skillet or crêpe pan. Brush with some melted butter, then add just enough batter to coat the pan with the thinnest possible layer. Pour off any extra batter, then cook for a few minutes, until the bottom is lightly brown and the edges curl. Turn with a spatula, then cook for a few minutes on the other side. Remove from the pan. Brush the pan with more melted butter before cooking the next crêpe. Proceed until all the batter is used.

MEAT FILLING FOR TWO CRÊPES

½ small onion, chopped
1 teaspoon oil
¼ pound ground beef
⅓ cup tomato sauce
1 large pimiento, chopped
½ beef bouillon cube
Salt
Freshly ground pepper
Pinch of basil
Pinch of oregano or marjoram
2 crêpes
Melted butter
Freshly grated Parmesan cheese

Sauté the onion in the oil until soft. Add the beef and brown it, breaking it up with a fork; drain off any excess fat. Add the tomato sauce, pimiento, bouillon cube, salt, pepper, basil and oregano. Bring to a boil, then simmer, stirring occasionally, for about 20 minutes. Spoon half of the mixture onto each crêpe. Roll up the crêpes and place them, seam side down, in a buttered shallow baking dish. Brush with melted butter and sprinkle generously with cheese.

Before eating, heat for about 10 minutes in a preheated 450° oven, or until sizzling hot.

CHICKEN-AND-MUSHROOM FILLING FOR TWO CRÊPES

3–4 mushrooms, minced
½ small onion, minced
1½ tablespoons butter
Salt
Freshly ground pepper
½ cup cooked chicken, in small cubes
3½ tablespoons heavy cream
2 crêpes
Chopped parsley

Cook the mushrooms and onion in the butter, stirring occasionally, until tender and dry. Remove from the heat and combine with salt, pepper, chicken and 1½ tablespoons of the heavy cream. Spoon half of the filling onto each crêpe, roll them up and arrange them, seam side down, in a buttered shallow baking dish.

Before eating, pour the remaining 2 tablespoons of cream over them and bake in a preheated 400° oven until hot. Sprinkle with chopped parsley.

Whole-Wheat Cheese Blintzes

Eat these with sour cream or applesauce.

¼ pound cottage or pot cheese
1 egg, beaten
2 tablespoons sugar
Salt
Freshly ground pepper
2½ tablespoons cold water
2 tablespoons milk
¼ cup whole-wheat flour
1½ teaspoons oil
Melted butter

Mix the cheese with ½ of the beaten egg, the sugar, ⅛ teaspoon salt and some pepper; set aside. Put the water, milk, the remaining egg and a pinch of salt in the blender. Add the flour and oil and whirl at high speed for 1 minute. Scrape down the sides with a rubber spatula and whirl for another 30 seconds. (The batter should have the consistency of heavy cream. If too thick, add more water.)

Heat an 8-inch skillet and brush it with some melted butter. Add a little batter, tilt the pan quickly to coat the bottom, then pour off any excess batter. Cook over medium heat for 1 minute, or until the bottom is golden. Remove from the pan and repeat until all the batter is used; you should have 2 or 3 pancakes. Place about 2 tablespoons of the cheese mixture at one end of the cooked side. Turn in the sides, envelope fashion, then roll up from the filled end. Before eating, brown in butter.

DESSERTS

✧➧✿➧✿➧✿➧✿➧✿➧✿➧✿➧✿➧✿➧✿➧✿➧✿➧✿➧✿➧✿➧✿➧✿➧✿➧✿✿➧✧

DON'T SKIP DESSERT WHEN YOU ARE EATING ALONE: every good meal deserves a proper conclusion. If you are watching calories, choose fruit or some simple dessert recipe.

Although you would probably not serve them to a party of eight, certain desserts—like milk shakes and ice cream sodas—seem perfect when you are eating alone. Others—like layer cakes and pies—do not work well for one person. Even with adequate freezer space for leftovers, there will still be too much of one thing to cope with in a reasonable amount of time. Save cakes and pies for when you have a large dinner party. If you miss the pleasure of baking, try some of our cookie recipes: they are for refrigerator cookies, so that you can slice off just the right amount of dough at any time.

Quick Apple-Cheddar Crisp

½ cup applesauce
¼ teaspoon grated orange peel
⅛ teaspoon cinnamon
Pinch of nutmeg
2 tablespoons whole-wheat cereal flakes
2 tablespoons shredded Cheddar cheese

Preheat the oven to 350°.

Combine the applesauce, orange peel, cinnamon and nutmeg. Pour into a small baking dish. Mix the cereal and cheese and spread over the top. Bake for 20–25 minutes, or until the cheese melts. Eat while the crisp is still warm.

Baked Apple Sundae

1 baking apple
2 tablespoons water
¼ cup sugar
¼ teaspoon cinnamon
1 large scoop vanilla ice cream
2 tablespoons coarsely chopped walnuts

Preheat the oven to 350°.

Cut the apple in half lengthwise and remove the core; do not peel. Place, cut side up, in a small baking pan. Add the water to the pan. Mix the sugar and cinnamon together and sprinkle over the apple halves. Cover with foil and bake for about 45 minutes, or until tender. Remove the foil, turn the apple over, cover and bake for 10 minutes more. Let cool in the pan.

When you are ready for dessert, place the apple pieces, cut side up, in a dessert dish and spoon the baking syrup over them. Top with the ice cream and sprinkle with the walnuts.

Baked Rum Bananas

1 tablespoon butter
1 teaspoon lemon juice
1 banana, peeled and halved crosswise
1 tablespoon packed brown sugar
2½ teaspoons light rum
¼ cup heavy cream
1½ teaspoons confectioners' sugar

Preheat the oven to 350°.

Melt the butter with the lemon juice in a small baking dish in the oven. Place the banana halves in the dish and turn to coat with the butter mixture. Sprinkle with the brown sugar and bake for 20 minutes, basting once. Sprinkle with 2 teaspoons of the rum and bake for 1 minute more. Beat the cream in a small bowl, adding the confectioners' sugar and the remaining rum, until stiff peaks form. Spoon over the warm bananas and eat at once.

Blueberry French-Toast Shortcake

¾ cup blueberries
2 tablespoons maple syrup
⅛ teaspoon grated lemon peel
1 teaspoon lemon juice
1 egg
3 tablespoons milk
1½ teaspoons sugar
⅛ teaspoon vanilla
Pinch of cinnamon
Pinch of salt
2 slices day-old bread
1 tablespoon butter
¼ cup heavy cream
1 tablespoon chopped walnuts

Mix the blueberries, 1 tablespoon of the syrup, lemon peel and lemon juice and let stand at room temperature for ½ hour, stirring occasionally.

Beat together the egg, milk, sugar, vanilla, cinnamon and salt. Soak the bread in the egg mixture. Fry the bread slices in hot butter in a skillet, turning once, until golden brown.

Whip the cream, adding the remaining tablespoon of syrup, until soft peaks form. Fold in the blueberries. Place one slice of the toast on a plate, spoon half the blueberry-cream mixture onto it, top with the other slice of toast and spoon the remaining blueberry mixture over it. Sprinkle with walnuts and eat while the dish is warm.

Classic Banana Split

When you eat alone, there's no one to check up on you: you can indulge your sweet tooth from time to time with such classic confections as this lavish banana split.

1 ripe banana, peeled
Vanilla, chocolate and strawberry ice cream
Strawberries
Fudge sauce
Pineapple sauce
Sweetened whipped cream
Chopped walnuts

Split the banana in half lengthwise. Place the halves, cut side up, on a plate and top with 3 scoops of ice cream, one of each flavor. Spoon strawberries on top of the vanilla ice cream, fudge sauce on top of the chocolate ice cream, and pineapple sauce on top of the strawberry ice cream. Spoon whipped cream over all and sprinkle with chopped walnuts.

Chocolate Mousse

1 ounce semisweet chocolate pieces
1 egg, separated
½ teaspoon grated orange rind
1 tablespoon sugar
Sweetened whipped cream

Melt the chocolate in the top of a double boiler over hot water. Beat the egg yolk lightly and stir it into the chocolate. Heat for a few minutes over hot, not boiling, water. Add the orange rind and the sugar and let cool slightly.

Beat the egg white until stiff and fold it into the chocolate mixture. Pour into a dessert dish and chill for several hours. Spoon whipped cream on top before eating.

Crème Brulée

½ cup heavy cream
1½ teaspoons granulated sugar
1 egg yolk, slightly beaten
2 teaspoons superfine sugar

Heat the cream in a saucepan, then stir in the granulated sugar. Gradually add some of the hot cream to the beaten yolk, then stir the yolk into the remaining cream. Cook over low heat, stirring constantly, until thickened. Pour into an individual ramekin and chill.

About 1 hour before serving, spread the sugar over the cream. Broil about 4 inches from the heat, watching carefully, until the sugar melts and becomes crispy, about 4–6 minutes. Chill until ready to serve.

Dried Apricots and Ice Cream

2 ounces dried apricots
¼ cup orange juice
Softened vanilla ice cream

Combine the apricots and the orange juice. Cover and let stand, stirring several times, for 24 hours. When ready to eat, spoon into a dish and cover with a generous scoop of ice cream.

Dried-Fruit Compote

Make this in larger quantities if you wish. It will keep in the refrigerator almost indefinitely.

½ cup mixed dried fruit
½ lemon, orange or lime, sliced
½-inch cinnamon stick
Up to 2 tablespoons brown sugar (optional)

Put the dried fruit, lemon slices and cinnamon in a jar. Add some sugar if you wish, then cover all with boiling water. Cool. Cover the jar and refrigerate. This dessert will improve with age.

Pickled Peach Slices

½ cup sliced peaches
1 tablespoon sugar
1 tablespoon cider vinegar
1 whole clove
1 whole allspice
1-inch cinnamon stick

Put the peaches in a small bowl. Combine the sugar, vinegar, clove, allspice and cinnamon stick in a small saucepan, bring to a boil and then simmer for 5 minutes. Pour over the peaches, cover and chill overnight or longer.

Caramel Pear

1 pear, peeled and halved lengthwise
¼ cup water
¼ cup orange juice
1 tablespoon granulated sugar
2 tablespoons packed brown sugar
¼ teaspoon shredded orange peel
2 tablespoons sour cream

Scoop out the core from each pear half with a small spoon. Bring the water, orange juice and granulated sugar to a boil in a skillet. Add the pears, cut side down, cover and simmer for 15–20 minutes, or until fork-tender.

Remove the pears to a small baking pan, cut side up. Sprinkle with 1 tablespoon of the brown sugar and broil for 6–10 minutes, until the tops are bubbly and shiny. Sprinkle with the remaining tablespoon of brown sugar and broil until the sugar melts. Garnish with the orange peel and eat warm or cool with a dollop of sour cream on top.

Chocolate Raspberry Cream

Fresh raspberries, a true luxury, make a perfect treat for one.

¼ cup heavy cream
⅛ teaspoon vanilla extract
½ ounce sweet cooking chocolate, grated fine
½ cup fresh raspberries
1–2 teaspoons sugar

Whip the cream, adding the vanilla. Blend in the chocolate. Set aside a few raspberries as a garnish. Sprinkle sugar to taste on the remaining berries, then fold them into the cream. Spoon into a dessert dish, decorate with the remaining raspberries and chill thoroughly.

Quick Rice Pudding

⅓ cup instant rice
½ cup milk
1 tablespoon sugar
¼ teaspoon salt
Pinch of cinnamon
1–2 tablespoons raisins (optional)

Combine all the ingredients in a saucepan and bring to a boil, stirring occasionally. Remove from the heat, cover and let stand for 12–15 minutes, or until all the liquid is absorbed and the rice is tender.

Strawberries Chantilly

1 cup whole strawberries
⅓ cup heavy cream
2 tablespoons sweet cooking chocolate, grated
1 teaspoon confectioners' sugar
1 teaspoon light rum

Hull the berries and put them in a dessert plate. Whip the cream until foamy and slightly thickened. Fold in the chocolate, sugar and rum. Spoon over the berries as a sauce.

Yogurt and Cottage Cheese

2 ounces large-curd, cream-style cottage cheese
2 ounces fruit-flavored yogurt

Mix the cottage cheese and yogurt lightly, then spoon into a dessert dish and chill until ready to eat.

Zabaglione

1 egg yolk
2 tablespoons sugar
Pinch of salt
1½ tablespoons sherry or Marsala
½ teaspoon lemon juice

Put all the ingredients in the top of a double boiler over hot, not boiling water, and beat with a rotary or electric beater until the mixture is foamy and holds its shape. Spoon into a sherbet glass and eat it while it is still warm.

Banana Milk Shake

Simple, filling and nourishing.

1 ripe banana
1 cup milk
⅛ cup nonfat dry milk
¼ teaspoon vanilla
Pinch of salt
Pinch of nutmeg
3 ice cubes

Put all the ingredients in a blender or food processor and whirl until the liquid is frothy and the ice is well crushed. Pour into a tall glass and drink at once.

Peanut-Coffee Shake

½ cup cold strong coffee
½ cup vanilla ice cream
1 tablespoon peanut butter
1 tablespoon sugar, or to taste

Put all the ingredients in a blender or food processor and whirl at high speed until foamy. Pour into a tall glass and drink at once.

Strawberry Ice Cream Soda

⅓ cup frozen strawberries, or crushed, sweetened fresh strawberries
3 tablespoons milk
1 large scoop strawberry ice cream
Chilled carbonated water
Whipped cream (optional)

Put the strawberries, milk and strawberry ice cream in a large glass. Fill with carbonated water, and top with whipped cream if you wish.

Cream-Cheese Refrigerator Cookies

This recipe will make about 2 dozen cookies. You can freeze part of the dough or hold it all in the refrigerator for about 4–5 days, slicing off just the amount of cookies you want at any specific time.

¼ cup butter, softened
1½ ounces cream cheese, softened
½ teaspoon vanilla
½ cup flour
Orange marmalade

Beat the butter, cream cheese and vanilla with an electric beater until well blended. Gradually stir in the flour. Turn the dough out on a floured board and shape into a 6-inch log. Wrap in foil or waxed paper and chill for at least a few hours.

When ready to bake, cut ¼-inch slices, top each with ¼ teaspoon of marmalade and bake on ungreased cookie sheets in a preheated 350° oven for 15 minutes, or until the bottoms are lightly browned. Be careful not to over-bake.

Peanut-Butter Refrigerator Cookies

Like Cream-Cheese Refrigerator Cookies (above), these cookies make it possible to enjoy home baking when you live alone. The dough keeps well in the refrigerator or freezer, and you can slice off just the amount of cookies you want. This recipe will make about two dozen altogether.

¼ cup shortening
¼ cup smooth peanut butter
½ cup sugar
1 egg
½ teaspoon vanilla
⅔ cup flour
¼ teaspoon baking soda
¼ teaspoon salt
1 teaspoon milk

Cream the shortening with an electric beater. Add the peanut butter and sugar and continue to beat until fluffy. Beat in the egg and the vanilla. Combine the flour, baking soda and salt and add to the creamed mixture together with the milk. Shape into a roll 2 inches in diameter, wrap in waxed paper or foil and chill thoroughly.

When ready to bake, cut ⅛-inch slices and bake on greased cookie sheets in a preheated 350° oven for about 8 minutes.

Dessert Sauces

Here are three splendid sauces which will transform ice cream, pudding or plain packaged cake into very special desserts.

CHOCOLATE SAUCE

1 ounce unsweetened chocolate
⅓ cup milk
⅛ teaspoon salt
¾ cup sugar
1½ tablespoons light corn syrup
1 tablespoon butter
½ teaspoon vanilla

Melt the chocolate in the milk over very low heat, stirring constantly. Beat until smooth. Add the salt, sugar and corn syrup and cook, stirring occasionally, for 2 or 3 minutes. Stir in the butter and vanilla. You will have about 1 cup of sauce.

VANILLA SAUCE

¼ cup sugar
1½ teaspoons light cornstarch
½ cup boiling water
1 tablespoon butter
½ teaspoon vanilla
Pinch of salt

Mix the sugar and cornstarch in a small saucepan. Stir in the boiling water and simmer for 5 minutes. Stir in the butter, vanilla and salt. Use warm. You will have about ¾ of a cup.

APRICOT-BRANDY SAUCE

¾ cup apricot jam
¼ cup water
1½ tablespoons sugar
1 tablespoon apricot, peach or other brandy

Mix together in a small saucepan the jam, water and sugar. Simmer for 10 minutes, stirring frequently. Add the brandy and cook 1 minute more. You will have about 1 cup of sauce.

INDEX

Anchovy Sauce, Trout with, 126
Apple(s)
 -Cheddar Crisp, Quick, 228
 and Potatoes, Lamb Chop with,
  79
 Rings, Baked Ham Slice with, 97
 Rings, Sausage and, 101
 Sundae, Baked, 228–29
Apricot(s)
 -Brandy Sauce, 241
 Dried, and Ice Cream, 232–33
Artichoke, Lamb Chop with, 78
Avocado Bisque, 7–8

Bacon and Blue-Cheese Burger,
  42–43
Baked Apple Sundae, 228–29
Baked Chicken Quarter, 107
Baked Fish Fillet with Potato and
  Onion, 130–31
Baked Ham Slice with Apple
  Rings, 97
Baked Orange Chicken, 107–8
Baked Rum Bananas, 229
Banana(s)
 Milk Shake, 237
 Rum, Baked, 229
 Split, Classic, 231
Barbecue Sauce, 196
 Chinese, 198
Barbecued Chicken Legs, 112
Barbecued Lamb Chop, 77

Barbecued Meat on a Bun, 28–29
Barley, Chicken Livers and, 120–21
Bean Sprout(s)
 with Green Pepper, 147
 Hamburger, 53–54
 Soup, 11
Beans
 Green, in Herb Butter, 146
 Kidney, and Egg Salad, 171
 Skillet Frankfurters and, 63
Béarnaise Sauce, 194–95
Beef, 59–73
 in Burgundy, 71–72
 Charcoal-Broiled Tournedos, 70
 Club Steak with Onions, 69–70
 Juk, 72–73
 Liver Orientale, 73
 Minute Steak au Poivre, 69
 Roast, and Spicy Sour Cream
  Sandwich, 28
 Steak Kabobs, 70–71
 See also Hamburger
Beer
 Frankfurters Simmered in, 61
 Shrimp Cooked in, 141
Beets, Buttered, 147
Bigos, 83
Bisque
 Avocado, 7–8
 Cold Clam or Salmon, 19–20
Blintzes, Whole-Wheat Cheese,
  224

Blueberry French-Toast Shortcake,
230
Blue-Cheese
Bacon Burger, 42–43
Cottage-Cheese Dressing, 204
Boiled Lobster, 136
Bologna-Cheese Sandwich,
French-Toasted, 30
Borsch, Cold Buttermilk, 20
Braised Celery with Peanut Sauce,
149
Braised Chicken Livers with
Brown Rice, 121
Braised Pork Chop, 86
Breaded Pigs' Knuckles, 101
Broiled Cheese-Topped Chicken
Sandwich, 33
Broiled Cornish Hen, 119
Broiled Egg-Salad Sandwich, 36
Broiled Fish Steak, 126–27
Broiled Lemon Chicken, 109
Broiled Lobster, 136–37
Broiled Meat-Tomato-Cheese
Sandwich, 29
Broiled Mustard-and-Honey-
Glazed Chicken, 110
Broiled Salmon Steak with Lemon-
Dill Butter, 128
Broiled Tomato, 154
Broiled Tuna-Cheese Sandwich,
38–39
Brown Rice
Braised Chicken Livers with, 121
Pilaf, 180
Burgundy, Beef in, 71–72
Butter
-Garlic Dip, 198
Herb, Green Beans in, 146
Lemon, Sautéed Scallops with,
138–39
Lemon-Dill, Broiled Salmon
Steak with, 128
Maître d'Hôtel, 197
Buttered Beets, 147
Butterfly Shrimp, 140
Buttermilk Borsch, Cold, 20

Cabbage Sauté, 148
Caper Sauce, Tuna in, 133
Caramel Pear, 234

Carrot(s)
and Lamb Patty, 84
Mustard, 148–49
Soup, Creamy, 18
Casserole, Macaroni-Chicken-
Cheese, 183
Celery
Braised with Peanut Sauce, 149
Italian Stewed Pork with, 90
-Lemon Pork Chop, 88
Soup, Cream of, 8
Charcoal-Broiled Tournedos, 70
Cheddar-Apple Crisp, Quick, 228
Cheese
-Bologna Sandwich, French-
Toasted, 30
Chickpea, and Salami Platter,
172
Fondue Sandwich, 31
-Macaroni-Chicken Casserole,
183
-Meat-Tomato Sandwich,
Broiled, 29
Rabbit, 31–32
Risotto, 182–83
Scrambled Eggs with, 213
Toast, Onion Soup with, 13
-Topped Chicken Sandwich,
Broiled, 33
-Topped Frankfurters in Rolls,
59
-Tuna Sandwich, Broiled, 38–39
-Walnut Burger, 45
Whole-Wheat Blintzes, 224
See also names of cheeses
Cheeseburger de Luxe, 47
Chef's Salad, 161–62
Chicken, 105–18
Baked Quarter, 107
Barbecued Legs, 112
Breast Beau Séjour, 113–14
Breast Gruyère, 112–13
Broiled, Mustard-and-Honey
Glazed, 110
Broiled Cheese-Topped
Sandwich, 33
-Chutney Soup, 10
Club Sandwich, 33–34
Curried, 117
-Grape Salad, 163
with Green Peppers, 118

-Ham Rolls, 115–16
Lemon Broiled, 109
-Macaroni-Cheese Casserole, 183
-and-Mushroom Filling for
  Crêpes, 223
Orange Baked, 107–8
Pilaf, 116–17
and Rice Skillet, 111
Salad, Easy, 162
Sesame Fried, 110–11
Soup, 9
Victoria, 108–9
with Walnuts, 114–15
Chicken Liver(s), 106, 119–21
and Barley, 120–21
Braised, with Brown Rice, 121
Chopped, in Sandwich, 36–37
Potato, and Eggs, 211–12
Stroganoff, 119–20
Chickpea, Salami, and Cheese
  Platter, 172
Chili, North American, 55
Chili Porcupine Balls, 56
Chilled Yogurt-Cucumber Soup,
  20–21
Chinese Barbecue Sauce, 198
Chinese-Style Hamburger, 53
Chocolate
  Mousse, 231–32
  Raspberry Cream, 235
  Sauce, 240
Chopped Chicken-Liver Sandwich,
  36–37
Chutney-Chicken Soup, 10
Clam(s)
  Bisque, Cold, 19–20
  Sauce, Spaghetti with, 185
  Steamed, 135
Classic Banana Split, 231
Club Steak with Onions, 67–70
Codfish Steak, Poached, 127–28
Coffee-Peanut Butter Shake,
  237–38
Cold Buttermilk Borsch, 20
Cold Clam or Salmon Bisque,
  19–20
Cold Poached Salmon Steak, 129
Cold Salmon Platter, 167
Compote, Dried-Fruit, 233
Cookies, Refrigerator

Cream-Cheese, 238–39
Peanut-Butter, 239–40
Corn Meal Crusty Frankfurters, 62
Cornish Hen, Broiled, 119
Cottage-Cheese
and Blue-Cheese Dressing, 204
Noodles, 184
Yogurt and, 236
Cream of Celery Soup, 8
Cream-Cheese
Refrigerator Cookies, 238–39
Scrambled Eggs with, 213–14
-Tuna Sandwich, 39
Creamy Carrot Soup, 18
Creamy Mushroom Sauce, 195–96
Crème Brulée, 232
Crêpes, 207, 221–24
Chicken-and-Mushroom Filling
  for, 223
Meat Filling for, 222
Crusty Corn Dogs, 62
Cuban Eggs, 219–20
Cucumber(s)
Pickled, 160
-Yogurt Soup, Chilled, 20–21
Curried Chicken, 117
Curried Ham, 100
Curried Pork, 93

Deep-Fried Hamburger Sandwich,
  47–48
Desserts, viii, 227–41
Baked Apple Sundae, 228–29
Baked Rum Bananas, 229
Banana Milk Shake, 237
Blueberry French-Toast
  Shortcake, 230
Caramel Pear, 234
Chocolate Mousse, 231–32
Chocolate Raspberry Cream, 235
Classic Banana Split, 231
Cream-Cheese Refrigerator
  Cookies, 238–39
Crème Brulée, 232
Dried Apricots and Ice Cream,
  232–33
Dried-Fruit Compote, 233
Peanut-Butter Refrigerator
  Cookies, 239–40
Peanut-Coffee Shake, 237–38
Pickled Peach Slices, 233–34

Quick Apple-Cheddar Crisp, 228
Quick Rice Pudding, 235
Sauces for, 240–41
Strawberries Chantilly, 236
Strawberry Ice Cream Soda, 238
Yogurt and Cottage Cheese, 236
Zabaglione, 236–37
Dill
-Lemon Butter, Broiled Salmon
Steak with, 128
-Mustard Sauce, 201–2
Dillburger, 46
Double-Decker Burger, 44–45
Dressings, 193, 199–204
Cottage- and Blue-Cheese, 204
Green French, 202–3
Pimiento Vinaigrette, 202
Russian, 200
Tomato French, 204
Tuna Mayonnaise, 201
Vinaigrette, 203
See also Sauces
Dried Apricots and Ice Cream,
232–33
Dried-Fruit Compote, 233

Easy Chicken Salad, 162
Egg(s), 207–19
Benedict, 214
Chicken Livers, Potato and,
211–12
Cuban, 219–20
Eggburger, 34
Hard-Cooked, and Potato, 220
Hearty Omelet, 208
and Kidney-Bean Salad, 171
Mushroom Omelet, 208–9
Piperade, 212
and Rice, Spanish, 218–19
Sailor's Omelet, 210
-Salad Sandwich, Broiled, 36
Salami and, 211
Salmon Omelet, 210
-Sardine-Onion Platter, 168
Scrambled, with Cheese, 213
Scrambled, with Cream-Cheese,
213–14
Shirred, with Ham, 216–17
-Spinach Salad, 170–71
-Stuffed Tomato, 217–18
à la Suisse, 215

Swiss Cheese Omelet Sandwich,
35
Venetian, 216
Eggburger, 34
Eggdrop Soup, 10–11
Escarole-Lentil Soup, 16

Fettucini alla Romana, 190
Filberts, Hamburger with, 50
Fish and Shellfish, 125–42
Baked Fish Fillet with Potato
and Onion, 130–31
Boiled Lobster, 136
Broiled Fish Steak, 126–27
Broiled Lobster, 136–37
Broiled Salmon Steak with
Lemon-Dill Butter, 128
Butterfly Shrimp, 140
Cold Poached Salmon Steak, 129
Golden Fish Fillet, 130
Grilled Scampi, Venetian Style,
142
Haddock with Garlic Sauce,
132–33
Mornay, 131
Oyster Pan Roast, 138
Poached Cod Steak, 127–28
Provençale, 132
Salmon Patties, 134–35
Sautéed Scallops with Lemon
Butter, 138–39
Scallops en Brochette, 139
Shrimp Cooked in Beer, 141
Steamed Clams, 135
Steamed Mussels, 137
Trout with Anchovy Sauce, 126
Tuna in Caper Sauce, 133
Tuna with Rice and Peas, 134
See also names of seafood
Frankfurters, viii, 58–64
and Beans, Skillet, 63
Beer-Simmered, 61
in Blankets, 59
Cheese-Topped in Rolls, 59
Crusty Corn Dogs, 62
Garlic-Pickled, 61–62
with Pepper and Onion, 60
with Relish, 58
and Sauerkraut Goulash, 63–64
freezing foods, ix–xi

French Dressing
  Green, 202–3
  Tomato, 204
French Peas, 149–50
French-Toast Blueberry
  Shortcake, 230
French-Toasted Bologna-Cheese
  Sandwich, 30
Fruit, Dried, in Compote, 233

Garlic
  -Butter Dip, 198
  and Olive Oil, Spaghetti with,
    187
  -Pickled Frankfurters, 61–62
  Sauce, Haddock with, 132–33
Gazpacho Andaluz, 21
Glazed Ham Steak, 96
Golden Fish Fillet, 130
Goulash, Frankfurter and
  Sauerkraut, 63–64
Grape-Chicken Salad, 163
Green Beans in Herb Butter, 146
Green French Dressing, 202–3
Green Onion and Potato Salad, 164
Green Pepper(s)
  Bean Sprouts with, 147
  Chicken with, 118
  and Onion, Frankfurters with, 60
  and Onion Skillet, 150
  and Pepperoni, 102
  and Tomato Soup, 15
Grilled Scampi, Venetian Style, 142

Haddock with Garlic Sauce,
  132–33
Ham, 96–100
  Baked Slice with Apple Rings,
    97
  -Chicken Rolls, 115–16
  Curried, 100
  and Potato, Home-fried, 99
  Shirred Eggs with, 216–17
  Southern-Style Steak, 97–98
  Steak, Glazed, 96
  and Sweet Potato Skillet, 99–100
  -Zucchini Skillet, 98
Hamburgers, viii, 42–58
  Bean-Sprout, 53–54
  Blue-Cheese and Bacon, 42–43
  Cheeseburger de Luxe, 47

Cheese-Walnut, 45
Chili Porcupine Balls, 56
Chinese-Style, 53
Deep-Fried Sandwich, 47–48
Dillburger, 46
Double-Decker, 44–45
Eggburger, 34
  with Filberts, 50
Hawaiian, 49–50
North American Chili, 55
Peanut Balls, 58
  with Pepper and Onion, 49
Peppy Steak, 51
Piquant, 42
Salisbury Steak with Mushroom
  Sauce, 54–55
Savory, 43
Sesame, 46
Steak Tartare Sandwich, 48
Stroganoff, 57
Stuffed, 44
Teriyaki, 52
Hard-Cooked Eggs and Potato, 220
Hash, Tomato, 155
Hawaiian Hamburger, 49–50
Hearty Omelet, 208
Herb(s)
  Butter, Green Beans, 146
  Pilaf, 181
  Spaghetti with, 186
Hollandaise Sauce, 194
Home-fried Ham and Potatoes, 99
Honey-and-Mustard-Glazed
  Chicken, Broiled, 110
Hot Mushroom Sandwich, 37
Hungarian Pork Chop, 87

Ice Cream
  Dried Apricots and, 232–33
  Soda, Strawberry, 238
Iced Creamy Vegetable Soup, 22
Italian Spinach, 153
Italian Stewed Pork with Celery,
  90
Italian-Style Potato Salad, 166

Kidney Stew, Lamb, 85
Kidney-Bean and Egg Salad, 171
kitchen equipment, xi–xiii

Lamb, 77–85
    Barbecued Chop, 77
    Bigos, 83
    and Carrot Patty, 84
    Chop with Apples and Potatoes,
        79
    Chop with Artichoke, 78
    Kidney Stew, 85
    Shank Milanaise, 80
    Skillet Chop, 77
    Turkish Pilaf, 81
    in White Wine, 82
Lemon
    Broiled Chicken, 109
    Butter, Scallops Sautéed with,
        138–39
    -Celery Pork Chop, 88
    -Dill Butter, Broiled Salmon
        Steak with, 128
Lentil
    -Escarole Soup, 16
    Soup with Vegetables, 17
Liver, see Beef; Chicken Liver
Lobster
    Boiled, 136
    Broiled, 136–37

Ma Ho Pork, 94
Macaroni
    -Chicken-Cheese Casserole, 183
    Salad, Piquant, 160–61
Maître d'Hôtel Butter, 197
Marinade, Spicy, 199
Marinated Salmon Salad, 167–68
Mayonnaise, Tuna, 201
Meat, 67–102
    Baked Ham Slice with Apple
        Rings, 97
    Barbecued, on a Bun, 28–29
    Barbecued Lamb Chop, 77
    Beef in Burgundy, 71–72
    Beef Juk, 72–73
    Beef Liver Orientale, 73
    Bigos, 83
    Braised Pork Chop, 86
    Breaded Pigs' Knuckles, 101
    Charcoal-Broiled Tournedos, 70
    Club Steak with Onions, 69–70
    Curried Ham, 100
    Curried Pork, 93

Filling for Crêpes, 222
    freezing, x–xi
    Glazed Ham Steak, 96
    Ham-Zucchini Skillet, 98
    Home-fried Ham and Potato, 99
    Hungarian Pork Chop, 87
    Italian Stewed Pork with Celery,
        90
    Lamb and Carrot Patty, 84
    Lamb Chop with Apples and
        Potatoes, 79
    Lamb Chop with Artichoke, 78
    Lamb Kidney Stew, 85
    Lamb Shank Milanaise, 80
    Lamb in White Wine, 82
    Lemon-Celery Pork Chop, 88
    Ma Ho Pork, 94
    Minute Steak au Poivre, 69
    Mushroom-Veal Stew, 76
    Orange-Baked Pork Chop, 88–89
    Pepperoni and Peppers, 102
    Pork-Vegetable Skillet, 89
    Pork-Zucchini Stir-Fry, 91
    Sausage and Apple Rings, 101
    Savory Country-Style Ribs, 96
    Skillet Ham and Sweet Potato,
        99–100
    Skillet Lamb Chop, 77
    Southern-Style Ham Steak,
        97–98
    Steak Kabobs, 70–71
    Sweet and Pungent Pork, 92
    Sweet-and-Sour Spareribs, 95
    Tacos, 40–41
    -Tomato-Cheese Sandwich,
        Broiled, 29
    Turkish Lamb Pilaf, 81
    Veal Piccata, 74
    Veal Scaloppine with
        Mushrooms, 75
    See also names of meats
Milk Shake, Banana, 237
Minute Steak au Poivre, 69
Mousse, Chocolate, 231–32
Mushroom(s)
    -and-Chicken Filling for Crêpes,
        223
    Omelet, 208–9
    Rice, 179
    Sandwich, Hot, 37
    Sauce, Creamy, 195–96

Sauce, Salisbury Steak with, 54–55
Sautéed, 150–51
Soup, 12
in Sour Cream, 151
Veal Scaloppine with, 75
-Veal Stew, 76
Mussels, Steamed, 137
Mustard
Carrots, 148–49
-Dill Sauce, 201–2
-and-Honey-Glazed Chicken, Broiled, 110

Noodles
Cottage-Cheese, 184
Polonaise, 184–85
North American Chili, 55

Olive Oil and Garlic, Spaghetti with, 187
Omelet(s)
Hearty, 208
Mushroom, 208–9
Sailor's, 210
Salmon, 209
Swiss Cheese Sandwich, 35
Onion(s)
Club Steak with, 69–70
and Green Pepper, Frankfurters with, 60
Green-Pepper Skillet, 150
Hamburger with Pepper and, 49
and Potato, Baked Fish Fillet with, 130–31
and Potato Salad, 164
-Potato Soup, 14
-Sardine-Egg Platter, 168
Soup with Cheese Toast, 13
Orange
-Baked Chicken, 107–8
-Baked Pork Chop, 88–89
Oyster
Pan Roast, 138
Stew, 7

Pancakes
Potato, 152–53
Zucchini, 156
Pasta, 177–78, 183–90
Cottage-Cheese Noodles, 184

Fettucini alla Romana, 190
Macaroni-Chicken-Cheese Casserole, 183
Noodles Polonaise, 184–85
Spaghetti Carbonara, 186–87
Spaghetti with Fresh Tomato Sauce, 188
Spaghetti with Herbs, 186
Spaghetti with Olive Oil and Garlic, 187
Spaghetti with Tuna Sauce, 189
Spaghetti with White Clam Sauce, 185
Peach Slices, Pickled, 233–34
Peanut Butter
-Coffee Shake, 237–38
Hamburger Balls, 58
Refrigerator Cookies, 239–40
Sauce, Braised Celery with, 149
Pear, Caramel, 234
Peas
French, 149–50
and Rice, Tuna with, 134
Pepperoni and Peppers, 102
Peppers, see Green Pepper(s)
Peppy Hamburger Steak, 51
Piccata, Veal, 74
Pickled Cucumbers, 160
Pickled Peach Slices, 233–34
Pickled Turnips, 155
Pigs' Knuckles, Breaded, 101
Pilafs
Brown-Rice, 180
Chicken, 116–17
Herb, 181
Turkish Lamb, 81
Pimiento Vinaigrette Dressing, 202
Piperade, 212
Piquant Hamburger, 42
Piquant Macaroni Salad, 160–61
Poached Cod Steak, 127–28
Pork, 86–96
Braised Chop, 86
Curried, 93
Fried Rice, 182
Hungarian Chop, 87
Italian, Stewed with Celery, 90
Lemon-Celery Chop, 88
Ma Ho, 94
Orange-Baked Chop, 88–89
Savory Country-Style Ribs, 96

Sweet-and-Pungent, 92
Sweet-and-Sour Spareribs, 95
-Vegetable Skillet, 89
-Zucchini Stir-Fry, 91
Potato(es)
  and Apples, Lamb Chop with, 79
  Chicken Livers, and Eggs,
    211–12
  and Green-Onion Salad, 164
  and Ham, Home-fried, 99
  Hard-Cooked Eggs and, 220
  and Onion, Baked Fish Fillet
    with, 130–31
  -Onion Soup, 14
  Pancakes, 152–53
  Salad, Hungarian Style, 165
  Salad, Italian-Style, 166
  Stuffed, 152
Pudding, Quick Rice, 235
Purée, Zucchini, 18–19

Quick Apple-Cheddar Crisp, 228
Quick Rice Pudding, 235

Raspberry Chocolate Cream, 235
Refrigerator Cookies
  Cream-Cheese, 238–39
  Peanut-Butter, 239–40
Relish, Frankfurters with, 58
Rice, 177–83
  Brown, Braised Chicken Livers
    with, 121
  Brown-Rice Pilaf, 180
  Cheese Risotto, 182–83
  Chicken Pilaf, 116–17
  and Chicken Skillet, 111
  and Eggs, Spanish, 218–19
  Herb Pilaf, 181
  Mushroom, 179
  and Peas, Tuna with, 134
  Pork Fried, 182
  Pudding, Quick, 235
  Turkish Lamb Pilaf, 81
  Yellow, 179
Risotto, Cheese, 182–83
Roast Beef and Spicy Sour Cream
  Sandwich, 28
Rum Bananas, Baked, 229
Russian Dressing, 200

Sailor's Omelet, 210
Salads, 159–73
  Chef's, 161–62
  Chicken, Easy, 162
  Chicken-Grape, 163
  Chickpea, Salami and Cheese
    Platter, 172
  Cold Salmon Platter, 167
  Egg-Spinach, 170–71
  Green-Onion and Potato, 164
  Kidney-Bean and Egg, 171
  Marinated Salmon, 167–68
  Pickled Cucumbers, 160
  Piquant Macaroni, 160–61
  Potato, Hungarian Style, 165
  Potato, Italian-Style, 166
  Sardine-Onion-Egg Platter, 168
  Tuna-Stuffed Tomato, 169
  West Coast, 170
  Zucchini, 173
Salami
  Chickpea, and Cheese Platter,
    172
  and Eggs, 211
Salisbury Steak with Mushroom
  Sauce, 54–55
Salmon
  Bisque, Cold, 19–20
  Cold Poached Steak, 129
  Omelet, 209
  Patties, 134–35
  Platter, Cold, 167
  Salad, Marinated, 167–68
  Steak with Lemon-Dill Butter,
    Broiled, 128
Sandwiches, viii, 27–64
  Barbecued Meat on a Bun, 28–29
  Broiled Cheese-Topped Chicken,
    33
  Broiled Egg-Salad, 36
  Broiled Meat-Tomato-Cheese, 29
  Broiled Tuna-Cheese, 38–39
  Cheese Fondue, 31
  Cheese Rabbit, 31–32
  Chicken Club, 33–34
  Chopped Chicken-Liver, 36–37
  Eggburger, 34
  Frankfurters, viii, 58–64
  French-Toasted Bologna-Cheese,
    30
  Hamburgers, viii, 42–58

Hot Mushroom, 37
Meat Tacos, 40–41
Roast Beef and Spicy Sour
    Cream, 28
Swiss Cheese Omelet, 35
Thin-Boy, 32
Tuna Cream-Cheese, 39
Tuna Roll, 38
Tuna Tacos, 41
Walnut-Tuna, 40
Sardine-Onion-Egg Platter, 168
Sauces, 193–99
    Anchovy, Trout with, 126
    Apricot-Brandy, 241
    Barbecue, 196
    Béarnaise, 194–95
    Caper, Tuna in, 133
    Chinese Barbecue, 198
    Chocolate, 240
    Clam, Spaghetti with, 185
    Creamy Mushroom, 195–96
    Dessert, 240–41
    Fresh Tomato, Spaghetti with,
        188
    Garlic, Haddock with, 132–33
    Garlic-Butter Dip, 198
    Hollandaise, 194
    Maître d'Hôtel Butter, 197
    Mushroom, Salisbury Steak with,
        54–55
    Mustard-Dill, 201–2
    Peanut, Braised Celery with, 149
    Spicy Marinade, 199
    Sweet-and-Sour, 197
    Tartar, 200
    Tuna, Spaghetti with, 189
    Vanilla, 241
    See also Dressings
Sauerkraut and Frankfurter
    Goulash, 63–64
Sausage and Apple Rings, 101
Sautéed Mushrooms, 150–51
Sautéed Scallops with Lemon
    Butter, 138–39
Sautéed Zucchini, 156
Savory Country-Style Ribs, 96
Savory Hamburger, 43
Scallops
    en Brochette, 139
    Sautéed, with Lemon Butter,
        138–39

Scaloppine, Veal with Mushrooms,
    75
Scampi, Grilled Venetian Style, 142
Scrambled Eggs with Cheese, 213
Scrambled Eggs with Cream
    Cheese, 213–14
Sesame Burger, 46
Sesame Fried Chicken, 110–11
Shellfish, see Fish and Shellfish;
    names of shellfish
Shirred Eggs with Ham, 216–17
Shortcake, Blueberry French-
    Toast, 230
Shrimp
    Butterfly, 140
    Cooked in Beer, 141
    Grilled Scampi, Venetian Style,
        142
Skillet Frankfurters and Beans, 63
Skillet Ham and Sweet Potato,
    99–100
Skillet Lamb Chop, 77
Soups, viii, 5–23
    Avocado Bisque, 7–8
    Chicken, 9
    Chicken-Chutney, 10
    Chilled Yogurt-Cucumber, 20–21
    Cold Buttermilk Borsch, 20
    Cold Clam or Salmon Bisque,
        19–20
    Cream of Celery, 8
    Creamy Carrot, 18
    Eggdrop, 10–11
    Escarole-Lentil, 16
    freezing, x
    Gazpacho Andaluz, 21
    Iced Creamy Vegetables, 22
    Lentil with Vegetables, 17
    Mushroom, 12
    Onion, with Cheese Toast, 13
    Onion-Potato, 14
    Oyster Stew, 7
    Spring, 11
    Sprout, 11
    Tomato and Green Pepper, 15
    Watercress, 22–23
    Zucchini Purée, 18–19
Sour Cream
    Mushrooms in, 151
    and Roast Beef Spicy Sandwich,
        28

Southern-Style Ham Steak, 97–98
Spaghetti
  Carbonara, 186–87
  with Fresh Tomato Sauce, 188
  with Herbs, 186
  with Olive Oil and Garlic, 187
  with Tuna Sauce, 189
  with White Clam Sauce, 185
Spanish Eggs and Rice, 218–19
Spareribs
  Savory Country-Style, 96
  Sweet-and-Sour, 95
Spicy Marinade, 199
Spinach
  -Egg Salad, 170–71
  Italian, 153
Spring Soup, 11
Sprout Soup, 11
Steak
  Broiled Salmon, with Lemon-
    Dill Butter, 128
  Club, with Onions, 69–70
  Cold Poached Salmon, 129
  Fish, Broiled, 126–27
  Ham, Glazed, 96
  Ham, Southern Style, 97–98
  Kabobs, 70–71
  Minute, au Poivre, 69
  Peppy Hamburger, 51
  Poached Codfish, 127–28
  Salisbury with Mushroom Sauce,
    54–55
  Tartare, in Sandwich, 48
Steamed Clams, 135
Steamed Mussels, 137
Stews
  freezing, x
  Lamb Kidney, 85
  Oyster, 7
  Veal-Mushroom, 76
Strawberry(ies)
  Chantilly, 236
  Ice Cream Soda, 238
Stroganoff
  Chicken Livers, 119–20
  Hamburger, 57
Stuffed Hamburger, 44
Stuffed Potato, 152
Succotash, 154
Sweet Potato and Ham Skillet,
  99–100

Sweet-and-Pungent Pork, 92
Sweet-and-Sour Sauce, 197
Sweet-and-Sour Spareribs, 95
Swiss Cheese Omelet Sandwich, 35

Tacos
  Meat, 40–41
  Tuna, 41
Tartar Sauce, 200
Teriyaki Burger, 52
Thin-Boy Sandwich, 32
Tomato
  Broiled, 154
  Egg-Stuffed, 217–18
  French Dressing, 204
  and Green-Pepper Soup, 15
  Hash, 155
  -Meat-Cheese Sandwich, Broiled,
    29
  Sauce, Spaghetti with, 188
  Tuna-Stuffed, 169
Tournedos, Charcoal-Broiled, 70
Trout with Anchovy Sauce, 126
Tuna
  in Caper Sauce, 133
  -Cheese Sandwich, Broiled,
    38–39
  Cream-Cheese Sandwich, 39
  Mayonnaise, 201
  with Rice and Peas, 134
  Sandwich Roll, 38
  Sauce, Spaghetti with, 189
  -Stuffed Tomato, 169
  Tacos, 41
  -Walnut Sandwich, 40
Turkish Lamb Pilaf, 81
Turnips, Pickled, 155

utensils, xi–xiii

Vanilla Sauce, 241
Veal, 74–76
  -Mushroom Stew, 76
  Piccata, 74
  Scaloppine with Mushrooms, 75
Vegetable(s), 145–56
  Bean Sprouts with Green
    Pepper, 147
  Braised Celery with Peanut
    Sauce, 149
  Broiled Tomato, 154

Buttered Beets, 147
Cabbage Sauté, 148
French Peas, 149–50
Green Beans in Herb Butter, 146
Green-Pepper and Onion Skillet, 150
Italian Spinach, 153
Lentil Soup with, 17
Mushrooms in Sour Cream, 151
Mustard Carrots, 148–49
Pickled Turnips, 155
-Pork Skillet, 89
Potato Pancakes, 152–53
Sautéed Mushrooms, 150–51
Sautéed Zucchini, 156
Soup, Iced Creamy, 22
Stuffed Potato, 152
Succotash, 154
Tomato Hash, 155
Zucchini Pancakes, 156
See also names of vegetables
Venetian Eggs, 216
Vinaigrette Dressing, 203
Pimiento, 202

Walnut
-Cheese Burger, 45
Chicken, 114–15
-Tuna Sandwich, 40
Watercress Soup, 22–23
West Coast Salad, 170
White Clam Sauce, Spaghetti with, 185
White Wine, Lamb in, 82
Whole-Wheat Cheese Blintzes, 224

Yellow Rice, 179
Yogurt
and Cottage Cheese, 236
-Cucumber Soup, Chilled, 20–21

Zabaglione, 236–37
Zucchini
-Ham Skillet, 98
Pancakes, 156
-Pork Stir-fry, 91
Purée, 18–19
Salad, 173
Sautéed, 156